Estate Planning in Louisiana

What others are saying about this book:

Paul Rabalais does a great job making complicated legal strategies simple. I recommend this book and his services to all of my clients who need estate planning help.
> - Macallyn J. Achee, Baton Rouge, LA attorney

Paul takes complicated legal topics and describes them in a way that makes them simple enough for anyone to understand.
> - Marcel Dupre, attorney and Chief Investment Officer, ThirtyNorth Investments, LLC

As someone who provides estate planning legal services in Louisiana, I recommend this book to any individual who wants to learn more about this important topic.
> - Doug White, Shreveport, LA attorney

I no longer provide estate planning services to clients. I refer clients who need estate planning legal services to Paul.
> - G. Steven Duplechain, Baton Rouge, LA attorney

Everyone who lives in Louisiana and wants to protect their estate for themselves and their family should read this book.
> - James Pope, CPA

Estate Planning in *Louisiana*

A Layman's Guide To Understanding
Wills, Trusts, Probate, Power of Attorney,
Medicaid, Living Wills, and Taxes

Third Edition

Paul A. Rabalais

Estate Planning for Life, LLC
Baton Rouge, Louisiana

Paul A. Rabalais is an attorney certified as a Specialist in Estate Planning and Administration by the Louisiana State Bar Association. He earned his law degree from the Louisiana State University Law Center, and his Master's Degree in Tax Law from the Boston University Law Center. He is the founder and President of Rabalais Law which has served thousands of clients since 1995.

Published by: Estate Planning for Life, LLC
9191 Siegen Lane, Unit 5B
Baton Rouge, LA 70810
© 2013 by Paul A. Rabalais
First edition published 2007. Second edition 2011. Third edition 2013.

ISBN-13, 978-0-9793982-1-6
ISBN-10, 0-9793982-1-5
First Printing 2007
Printed in the United States of America

20 19 18 17 16 15 14   2 3 4 5

Library of Congress Cataloging-in-Publication Data
Rabalais, Paul.
Estate Planning in Louisiana: A Layman's Guide To Understanding Wills, Trusts, Probate, Power of Attorney, Medicaid, Living Wills, and Taxes/Paul A. Rabalais.
— 3rd ed.
ISBN-13, 978-0-9793982-1-6
ISBN-10, 0-9793982-1-5

To my wife, Amy, and our five children: Andrew, Taylor, Connor, William, and Anna Claire

Contents

About the Author   xi
Acknowledgments   xii
Warning – Disclaimer   xiii

1   Estate Planning in Louisiana   1
     Why Is Everything so Different?

2   Louisiana Community Property   9
     Marriage Is an Equal Partnership – Sort of

3   Forced Heirship   17
     What If I Do Not Want to Leave It to My Kids?

4   Power of Attorney   23
     Who Will Take Care of Me and My Money?

5   Louisiana Intestate Laws   31
     What Happens When You Die without a Will?

6   Your Last Will and Testament   41
     Maybe the Most Important Document You Ever Sign

7   Protect Your Children and Grandchildren   53
     *How to Preserve Your Assets from Taxes, Long-Term
     Care Costs, and Your Children's Divorces and Poor
     Spending Habits*

8   Multiple Marriages   65
     *Protect Your Second Spouse AND Your Children from
     Your First Spouse*

9   Death and Taxes   79
     Benjamin Franklin Said It Best

10   Usufruct   91
     What in the Heck Is a Usufruct?

11   Living Wills   103
     Making Your Wishes Known about Life Support
     Machines

12   Trusts   109
     Trusts Can Be Great Tools - When Used for the Right
     Reasons

13   Medicaid Planning   129
     Avoid Nursing Home Poverty

14   Successions and Probate   145
     Handling Legal Matters When a Loved One Dies

15   Non-probate Assets   163
     These Are Important and Often Overlooked

16   Estate Planning Letter of Last Instructions   169
     Make It Easy for Your Loved Ones

17   Get Started   173
     It's Not as Painful as You Might Think

Glossary   179

About the Author

Paul A. Rabalais discovered the benefits of estate planning at an early age. At the age of eight, he received an inheritance from his grandmother. The fruits of his inheritance helped him pay for his college and law school education.

In 1987, Paul graduated from Louisiana State University with a degree in Finance. In 1990, he earned his law degree from LSU Law School.

Paul furthered his knowledge of estate planning and the federal tax system by earning a Master's Degree in Tax Law from Boston University School of Law in 1991.

From 1991 through 1994, Paul worked for some of the top law firms in the state of Louisiana. In early 1995, Paul started his own estate planning law firm.

Paul has provided estate planning legal services to thousands of clients through his law firm. He has written numerous articles on various aspects of estate planning, and he has given hundreds of seminars on estate planning.

Paul can be contacted by email at paul@rabalaislaw.com

Acknowledgments

I have not attempted to cite in the text all of the authorities and sources consulted in the preparation of this book. To do so would require more space than is available. The list would include departments of the parish, state and federal government, libraries, Web sources, and numerous individual clients.

Special thanks goes to Catherine Martinez, who helped me arrange to have enough uninterrupted free time to be able to write this book.

Special thanks to all of our law firm's clients who we have been so fortunate to serve. It has been a pleasure for 20 years to go to work every day helping to improve and enhance the relationships of the families that we serve.

Angela Farley provided a great cover design.

Disclaimer

This book is designed to provide information about the subject matter covered. If you require legal, accounting or other professional assistance, the services of a competent professional should be sought.

Every effort has been made to make this book as complete and as accurate as possible. However, there may be mistakes both typographical and in content. Therefore, this text should be used only as a general guide and not as the ultimate source of estate planning law in Louisiana. Further, this book contains information on estate planning only up to the printing date.

The purpose of this book is to educate and entertain. The author shall have neither liability nor responsibility to any person or entity with respect to any loss or damage caused or alleged to be caused directly or indirectly by the information contained in this book.

If you do not wish to be bound by the above, you may return this book to the publisher for a full refund.

Chapter 1

Estate Planning in Louisiana
Why Is Everything so Different?

You have all heard of the phrase, "Getting your affairs in order." Well, that is a simple but effective definition of estate planning.

You do not know when you are going to die. You do not know if you will be incapacitated during your lifetime. As a result of that uncertainty, you need to plan.

The purpose of this book is to educate you, the lay person, about estate planning. This book is specifically designed to benefit you if you live in the State of Louisiana. When it comes to estate planning, Louisiana laws are different from the laws of all the other 49 states.

Estate Planning Involves Protecting What You Own

You have probably worked hard to accumulate what you have. If you do not plan properly your assets can be taken away. For example, if you go into a nursing home, you could spend thousands of dollars each month on your care. Or if you do not handle your retirement account properly, you could pay unnecessary income tax. If you do not plan for your future incapacity, your estate could be squandered away in a court-supervised guardianship proceeding. With all the lawsuits in America today, it is even possible that you could be successfully sued resulting in someone taking your entire estate away from you.

So, you can protect what you own while you are alive by:
- Protecting your assets from nursing home expenses;
- Minimizing your income tax;
- Avoiding a court-supervised guardianship proceeding in the event of your incapacity, and
- Protecting your assets if you are sued.

Estate Planning Includes Taking Action to Protect Your Surviving Spouse

You may be thinking that you want to make sure your husband or wife has financial security when you die. The Louisiana laws that apply when a married person dies benefit the children more than the surviving spouse. It is important for you to take action to give your surviving spouse the security he or she needs.

Example. Bob inherited stock in ABC, Inc. from his parents. Bob and his wife, Mary, are using the dividends from the stock to pay their monthly expenses. While Bob knows that he would want Mary to continue receiving dividends from the stock if Bob dies first, he never takes any action (such as getting his Last Will and Testament written) to protect Mary.

Because Bob had taken no action to protect Mary, all of the stock Bob had inherited went to Bob's children when he died unexpectedly, and Mary was left with nothing.

Louisiana law is unique when it comes to what the surviving spouse can do with the family home after one spouse dies. In most instances, if a surviving wife wants to sell the home in which she lived with her husband, she has to get the written permission of all of his children to sell the home. You may be thinking that you and your spouse worked hard to pay for the home and you should not have to get the permission of your children (or your spouse's children) in order to sell your home. You can plan ahead to avoid these problems.

Proper planning can even prevent your children from forcing your spouse to sell his or her house after you die. Again, the laws that apply in Louisiana when you die without planning typically favor the children over the surviving spouse.

Estate planning can protect your spouse by:

- Arranging for your assets to be available for your spouse after you die (as opposed to going straight to your children or to others);

- Arranging your affairs so your spouse will have the freedom to sell your home, other real estate, or other assets after you die (without having to get the permission of your children); and

- Eliminating the possibility that your children could force your spouse to sell assets or pay them their inheritance immediately.

Estate Planning Involves Taking Action to Protect Your Children

You have worked hard over your lifetime raising your children and providing financial security for yourself and, if you are married, for your spouse. You may be thinking that you would like to be able to provide one final gift to your children by leaving them an inheritance. How nice would that be to allow your children to have peace of mind in their remaining years because you were able to leave them an inheritance?

Or maybe you ride around in your car with one of those bumper stickers that reads, "I'm spending my children's inheritance." While that may be true, I will bet that you would rather have your children (or some other loved ones) inherit from you as opposed to your assets going to the government, the lawyers, or the courts.

Leaving assets to your children can be complex. Whether your children are young or old, rich or poor, married or single, you need to be aware of some important legal concepts that could jeopardize your children's inheritance.

If your children are young, you would better have an estate plan. If you die before your children reach the age of 18 and you do not have a properly written Last Will and Testament, a judge will determine who will raise your children until they reach the age of 18. In addition, a judge will determine who will control any financial assets that your children inherit, and if any of those assets need to be spent on your children before they reach the age of 18 (for school expenses, living expenses, etc.), a judge will have to approve each expenditure. This tutorship procedure is complicated and expensive.

If your children are married, have been married, or even if they might get married in the future, you need to take action to protect their inheritance from their past or future divorces. You already know that many marriages these days end in divorce. What you may not know, however, is that if your children inherit from you and then get divorced, your child may have to share that inheritance with their ex-spouse.

You can also protect your children by arranging to minimize the tax they pay at your death. A federal estate tax exists that could require your children to pay up to half of their inheritance to the IRS. Capital gains tax and income tax can also be minimized or avoided through proper estate planning.

If you have children from a prior marriage, estate planning is a must. It is common for children to get nothing because their step-parent receives all the assets.

Example. James had three children from his first marriage to First Wife. James and First Wife divorced. James later married Second Wife. When James died, all of his assets went to Second Wife. James' three children from his marriage to First Wife received nothing. When Second Wife later died, Second Wife left all of her assets (including the assets she received from James) to Second Wife's children.

Proper estate planning can avoid these problems. James could have arranged his estate plan to provide for Second Wife but also provided that at Second Wife's subsequent death, assets would revert back to James' children.

Take action to protect your children:

- If your children are minors (or if they are 18 or over but unable to manage money to your standards), set up your estate plan so the court supervised guardianship proceeding is avoided and you dictate who raises your children and who handles their inheritance;
- If your children are older, take action to avoid leaving assets to your daughter-in-law or your son-in-law, particularly if your children have been divorced or may get divorced in the future;
- Arrange your affairs to avoid unnecessary taxes; and
- Protect the inheritance for your children - even if you are in a second marriage and you and your spouse each have children from a prior marriage.

What Makes Estate Planning in Louisiana so Different?

Louisiana laws, as they relate to estate planning, are unique. Louisiana derives its laws from the French

Paul A. Rabalais

Napoleonic Code, unlike all other states. Many of the national articles or publications that you read about estate planning simply do not apply to Louisiana residents.

Louisiana is one of a handful of community property states. In general, what this means is that a marriage is treated as an equal partnership. For example, if the husband starts and builds a business that is titled in his name only, and his wife stays home and raises their children, each spouse is deemed to own one-half of the business, even though it is titled in the husband's name and even though he was the one who built the business.

Louisiana is the only state that has forced heirship laws. Many people are confused about Louisiana's forced heirship laws. These laws provide that you cannot disinherit certain children. In general, if your children are 23 years of age or younger, or if they are disabled (regardless of their age), they are forced heirs and you are going to have to leave them an inheritance. If you have one child, the amount you must leave that forced heir is one-fourth of your estate. If you have two or more children, you must leave them half of your estate. Remember, most parents want to leave their entire estate to their children so, in those instances, the forced heirship laws are not an issue.

The issue that confuses most people about Louisiana estate planning laws is the legal form of ownership called "usufruct." Usufruct exists only in Louisiana but it is a form of ownership very common in Louisiana. You will not read about usufruct in any national publications, books, or magazines since it is a Louisiana term. If you want to understand estate planning in Louisiana, you has better understand something about usufruct and naked ownership.

Often, when a married person dies, his or her surviving spouse inherits the usufruct of the deceased spouse's assets. This can be done through the Last Will and Testament of the person who died, or it can be done through the laws that apply when a person dies without a Last Will and Testament. The surviving spouse, as usufructuary, can generally "use" and "receive the fruits" from those assets, and at some later date - perhaps at her remarriage or her death - those assets will then belong to the naked owners.

Recognize that Louisiana laws are unique in that:

- Louisiana derives its laws from France;
- Louisiana is one of a handful of community property states;
- Louisiana is the only state that has forced heirship for certain children; and
- The form of ownership called "usufruct" is very common but used only in Louisiana.

Chapter 2

Louisiana Community Property
Marriage Is an Equal Partnership – Sort of

Louisiana is a community property state. Generally, each spouse owns one-half of all the community property. Our laws dictate what each spouse's rights and responsibilities are as relates to their community property.

Example. Ted and Ruth are married. They are each in their second marriage. Ted and Ruth, while they were married to each other, purchased a home, vehicles, and other community property. The vehicles were titled in Ted's name. Ted left a Last Will and Testament leaving his home and all of his vehicles to his son from his previous marriage, Fred. Since the home and vehicles were community property, Ruth keeps her one-half ownership interest in them, and Fred inherits only Ted's one-half ownership interest.

It is important to understand Louisiana's community property rules. When a married person dies or gets divorced, these rules dictate who owns what and govern each party's rights.

What Is Community Property?

The general concept behind community property is that all things acquired during a marriage by either spouse are owned one-half by each spouse regardless of who earned it or how it is titled.

Example. During their 30 year marriage, Steve earned wages while his wife, Jane, stayed home. Jane never worked outside the home. Thirty years after their marriage, Steve had an investment account with $2,000,000 of assets. Even though Steve earned the money, and even though the account was titled in his name only, the account is community property and Jane has a one-half ownership interest in the account.

Community Property Includes:

- Property acquired during the marriage through the effort, skill, or industry of either spouse,
- Property acquired with community things,
- Property donated to the spouses jointly,
- Damages awarded for loss or injury to a thing belonging to the community, and
- All other property not classified by law as separate property.

Separate Property Includes:

- Property acquired by a spouse prior to the marriage,

- Property acquired by a spouse with separate things or with separate and community things when the value of the community things is inconsequential in comparison with the value of the separate things used,
- Property acquired by a spouse by inheritance or donation to him or her individually, and
- Things acquired by a spouse as a result of a voluntary partition of the community during the existence of the community property regime.

Presumption of Community Property

Things a spouse has during the marriage are presumed to be community property, but either spouse may prove that they are separate property.

Fruits and Revenues of Separate Property

The natural and civil fruits of the separate property of a spouse, minerals produced from or attributable to a separate asset, and bonuses, delay rentals, royalties and shut-in payments arising from mineral leases are community property. For example, dividends produced by stock are community property even though the stock is the separate property of a spouse. Also, interest on savings accounts and certificates of deposit are community property even though the funds in those accounts are the separate property of a spouse.

A spouse, however, may sign a proper declaration reserving the fruits and revenues as his or her separate property. As to fruits and revenues from real estate owned as separate property by a spouse, this declaration is effective when a copy is provided to the other spouse and the declaration is recorded in the conveyance records of the parish where the real estate is located. As to fruits and revenues of other assets such as stock or cash owned as separate property by a spouse, the declaration is effective when a copy of the declaration is provided to the other spouse and the declaration is recorded in the parish in which the person signing the declaration is domiciled.

Unintentional Conversion from Separate Property to Community Property

Example. Jack and Jill are married. It is the second marriage for each of them. On the day they married, Jill had an investment account in her name that consisted of $500,000 worth of stocks, bonds, and cash. Her intent was that, at her death, this account would go to her three children from her first marriage. During the 15 years that she was married to Jack, the assets in the account produced a significant amount of interest and dividends. Also during her marriage to Jack, she made some deposits and took some withdrawals from this account. When Jack died 15 years after their marriage, Jill's account was valued at $850,000. Jack's heirs (his children) argued that this investment was community property (and one-half of the account should be in Jack's estate) since:
- The fruits and revenues (interest and dividends) are community property; and
- When community property and separate property get commingled so it is impossible to determine which assets are separate and which assets are community, then all assets become community.

Since Jack's Last Will and Testament left his entire estate to his two children from his first marriage, Jill may be forced to give one-half of her account to Jack's two children.

Jill could have avoided this problem by signing and recording a Declaration reserving the fruits and revenues from her separate property as her separate property. She could also have avoided these problems by entering into a matrimonial agreement with Jack prior to their marriage.

Matrimonial Agreements

Many couples, especially those with children from previous marriages, enter into a matrimonial agreement. These agreements are also commonly referred to as:

- Pre-nuptial agreements
- Marriage contracts
- Separate property agreements

Spouses are free to establish by matrimonial agreement an arrangement whereby there is no community property and all property is the separate property of the spouses. Spouses may also agree to modify the community property rules that we have in Louisiana.

Example. Pete and Gloria are getting married. They each have assets and income of their own. They enter into a matrimonial agreement prior to their marriage that states they will be separate in property. The agreement includes provisions stating that all assets earned or acquired by a spouse during the marriage, including any fruits and revenues, are the separate property of the spouse who earns or acquires the assets. If, in the previous example, Jack and Jill had entered into a proper matrimonial agreement prior to their marriage, then at Jack's death, Jill would have continued to own the entire $850,000 investment account.

Timeliness of Matrimonial Agreement

Prior to marriage, spouses may enter into a matrimonial agreement. During their marriage, spouses may, at any time, terminate their matrimonial agreement and subject themselves to the community property rules.

During their marriage, spouses may enter into a matrimonial agreement only by petitioning the court and upon a finding by the court that the matrimonial agreement serves their best interests and that the spouses understand the governing principles and rules.

During the first year after moving into and acquiring a domicile in this state, spouses may enter into a matrimonial agreement without court approval.

Claims for Reimbursement

When a spouse dies, a spouse (or their estate) may have a claim for reimbursement against the other spouse (or their estate).

Example. Two years prior to the marriage of Rod and Beth, Rod purchased a home for $200,000. He paid $20,000 as a down payment and financed $180,000 on a 30 year mortgage. Twenty years after they married (with eight years of payments left), Rod died. Since the home was purchased prior to the marriage, the home is Rod's separate property. However, since community property was used to pay the mortgage payments, Beth is entitled to be reimbursed from Rod's estate for one-half of the total mortgage payments made during their marriage.

If community property has been used to satisfy a separate obligation of a spouse, the other spouse or his heirs are entitled to reimbursement upon termination of the community property regime for one-half of the amount of the money used.

If a spouse uses his own separate property to satisfy a community debt, then upon the death of a spouse, he (or his estate) is entitled to reimbursement for one-half of the amount used.

Retirement Accounts and Community Property

Different rules apply to retirement accounts such as 401(k) accounts and Individual Retirement Accounts (IRAs).

Example. Ted was employed at a company for 35 years and built up his 401(k) so that when he retired, it was worth $800,000. When he retired, he rolled over his 401(k) into an IRA. When Ted's wife, Alice, died, Ted's entire IRA stayed in his name while Alice's Will controlled the disposition of her half of all the other community property they acquired during their marriage. Even though the funds in the IRA were acquired during Ted's marriage to Alice, those funds will stay in Ted's name. When Ted later dies, the funds will be distributed to the persons designated on Ted's beneficiary designation form. Neither Ted's nor Alice's Will controls the disposition of Ted's IRA.

If, in the previous example, Ted and Alice divorced, then the IRA would be split and it would be treated as community property. The rules are different when a married IRA owner dies. IRAs cannot be put in the names of both spouses.

Conclusion

If you are married and you live in Louisiana, you are subject to the Louisiana community property laws which essentially provide that anything you and your spouse acquire during your marriage is owned one-half by each of you. You will want to remember that:

- Anything you or your spouse earn during your marriage is community property. It does not matter who earned it and it does not matter in whose name it is titled;
- Property you acquire by gift or inheritance or property you owned before you married is your separate property;
- Income from your separate property is community property; and
- You can enter into a matrimonial agreement with your spouse to deviate from the Louisiana community property rules.

Chapter 3

Forced Heirship
What If I Do Not Want to Leave It to My Kids?

Louisiana is unique in that it has forced heirship laws. Forced heirship has meant, over the years, that your children are automatically entitled to inherit from you, regardless of what you put in your Will.

Example. Fred and Sally are married. Fred has two children who are classified as forced heirs. Fred's Will leaves everything he owns at his death to his wife, Sally. Fred's Will violates the forced heirship provisions. Fred's two children have a right to demand their forced portion from Fred's estate.

Many people confuse the forced heirship laws with the intestate laws. If you die intestate (without a Will), your entire estate will go to your children, but your surviving spouse will have a usufruct over your half of the community property. The forced heirship laws apply when you write a Will but leave all or the bulk of your estate to someone other than your forced heirs.

Estate Planning in Louisiana

Who Is a Forced Heir?

In the past, all of your children were considered forced heirs. On October 21, 1995, Louisiana voters approved an amendment to the Constitution of Louisiana, dealing with forced heirship.

Forced heirs are now defined, in general, as your children who, at the time of your death, are 23 years of age or younger, or your children of any age who, because of mental incapacity or physical infirmity, are permanently incapable of taking care of their persons or administering their estates at the time of your death.

For purposes of the forced heirship rules, the definition of "permanently incapable of taking care of their persons and administering their estates at the time of the death of the decedent" includes your children who, at the time of your death, have medical documentation showing an inherited, incurable disease or condition that may render them incapable of caring for themselves or their estates in the future.

If your child dies before you, your child's children are forced heirs if, at the time of your death, your child would have been 23 years of age or younger. However, if your child predeceases you, and your child has a child who, because of mental incapacity or physical infirmity, is permanently incapable of taking care of his or her person or administering his or her estate, then that grandchild is a forced heir regardless of how old your child would have been at the time of your death.

What Is the Forced Portion?

In general, if you have one forced heir at the time of your death, that forced heir is entitled to one-fourth of your estate. If you have two or more forced heirs at the time of your death, they are entitled to split one-half of your estate. The portion that must go to your forced heirs is called the forced portion. The remainder of your estate (that you can leave to anyone you wish) is called the disposable portion.

Life insurance proceeds and most retirement account balances (such as 401(k)s and IRAs) are not counted when calculating the forced portion. However, the value of those benefits paid to a forced heir will be credited toward his forced portion.

Example. Jim died with one forced heir, a son who was 22 at the time of Jim's death. Jim's Will left his entire estate to his new wife, Anna. Anna was also named as the beneficiary of Jim's $500,000 life insurance policy and Jim's $400,000 IRA. Jim owned other assets worth $200,000 at the time of his death. Generally, Jim's estate owes $50,000 (1/4 of $200,000) to Jim's forced heir.

Usufruct to Your Surviving Spouse

You may leave your surviving spouse the usufruct of the forced portion. The usufruct may last for the lifetime of the surviving spouse.

Example. Tony died with two children, ages 19 and 22. In Tony's Will, he bequeathed to his children their forced portion (one-half of his estate to be divided equally between them), but he bequeathed to his wife, Rachel, the usufruct of the forced portion for the remainder of her lifetime. Tony bequeathed the remainder of his estate (the remaining one-half) to Rachel in full ownership. This is permissible.

Can You Disinherit a Forced Heir?

If you have a child who is 22 years of age, then he or she is a forced heir. However, there are eight different just causes for disinherison. You must expressly state the cause in your Will, and you must identify who you are disinheriting. A parent has just cause to disinherit a child if:

1. The child has raised his hand to strike a parent, or has actually struck a parent; but a mere threat is not sufficient.
2. The child has been guilty, towards a parent, of cruel treatment, crime, or grievous injury.
3. The child has attempted to take the life of a parent.
4. The child, without any reasonable basis, has accused a parent of committing a crime for which the law provides that the punishment could be life imprisonment or death.
5. The child has used any act of violence or coercion to hinder a parent from making a testament.
6. The child, being a minor, has married without the consent of the parent.
7. The child has been convicted of a crime for which the law provides that the punishment could be life imprisonment or death.

8. The child, after attaining the age of majority and knowing how to contact the parent, has failed to communicate with the parent without just cause for a period of two years, unless the child was on active duty in any of the military forces of the United States at the time.

For a disinherison to be valid, the cause must have occurred prior to the execution of the Will that disinherits the heir.

Conclusion

If you live in Louisiana, you are subject to our unique forced heirship laws which require that certain children are automatically entitled to inherit from you. In general:

- Forced heirs are children 23 years of age or younger, or children of any age who are incapacitated;
- If you have one forced heir, that forced heir is entitled to one-fourth of your estate. If you have two or more forced heirs, those forced heirs are entitled to share one-half of your estate;
- Life insurance and most retirement accounts are not counted for purposes of forced heirship;
- You can expressly disinherit a forced heir for one of eight just causes.

Chapter 4

Power of Attorney
Who Will Take Care of Me and My Money?

What is a power of attorney? A power of attorney is a document that you sign that gives someone else (your Agent) the authority to act for you under certain circumstances.

Example. Ronald has two children, Adam and Eve. Ronald wants Adam to handle Ronald's affairs for him if Ronald ever becomes incapacitated. Ronald signs a power of attorney authorizing Adam to handle all of Ronald's financial affairs.

Why is a power of attorney important? If you do not sign a power of attorney and you become incapable of managing your own affairs during your lifetime, either by accident, illness, or other incapacity, there will likely be a court-supervised interdiction proceeding whereby you and your closest relatives will be at the mercy of the court. The court will, after considerable time and expense, pick a curator whose job it will be to manage your affairs and report to the court for permission to act on your behalf and for other matters. The interdiction is a burden that can be avoided.

Estate Planning in Louisiana

Many people mistakenly believe that estate planning only involves getting their Last Will and Testament in place. Your Will does nothing for you in the event you become incapacitated during your lifetime. You need to make certain that you have the proper power of attorney documents in place. Laws in Louisiana regarding your power of attorney differ from the power of attorney laws of all the other states.

Why Have a Power of Attorney?

There are many reasons that you should sign a properly drafted power of attorney as part of your estate plan:

- You will likely avoid the burdensome court-supervised interdiction proceeding that may be necessary when you become incapacitated and you have not executed a proper power of attorney;
- You can designate the person who will handle your affairs for you if you become incapacitated;
- If an interdiction is necessary, you can designate in your power of attorney who you would want the court to designate as your curator or legal guardian during your incapacity;
- You can authorize your Agent in your power of attorney to engage in tax planning and Medicaid planning techniques that he or she would not be able to perform in an interdiction proceeding.

Paul A. Rabalais

Different Types of Power of Attorney

All powers of attorney are not the same. You need to make important decisions before you sign your power of attorney.

Limited power of attorney. You and your two sisters inherited your parents' house a year ago, and it is now on the market. Someone has agreed to buy the home but you are going to be out of town on the date the closing is to take place so you will not be available to sign on the Act of Sale. Two weeks before the closing, you sign a Limited Power of Attorney authorizing one of your sisters to act for you in the sale of the property. Your sister cannot take any other actions for you other than acting for you at the closing. Your sister signs her name as your Agent, and you receive your share of the proceeds of the sale of the home.

General power of attorney. While discussing your estate plan with your attorney, the attorney asks you who you would want to manage your affairs if at some point in the future you become incapacitated. Your attorney explains that most people execute a properly drafted power of attorney as part of their estate plan. He explains the benefits of avoiding the interdiction proceeding. You tell the attorney that you would want your spouse signing for you if you were unable to sign during your lifetime, and you state that you would want your oldest son to do it if your spouse were unable. Your attorney prepares a general power of attorney authorizing your spouse to act for you and providing that your son can act for you if your spouse has died or is otherwise unable to act for you.

If, for example, two years later you have a stroke and your house or vehicle need to be sold, it should be simple for your spouse (or your son if your spouse is unable) to sign the necessary documents allowing them to sell your assets if that is what is best for you.

Health Care Power of Attorney

You can designate in your health care power of attorney who you would want making your medical decisions for you if you are unable to make your own. You may have a living will whereby you declare your intentions regarding life-support machines, but your health care power of attorney covers other important medical decisions.

For example, let's say you are in surgery or have some other medical condition and you do not have the ability to properly communicate your wishes regarding medical treatment to your physicians. If you previously signed a health care power of attorney, the physician can rely on the Agent you named to make important treatment decisions for you.

When Is Your Power of Attorney Effective?

Your power of attorney that you sign will either be effective immediately or it will "spring" into effect at a later date.

Immediate Power of Attorney

If your power of attorney is effective immediately (and most are set up this way), then the person that you designated to act for you may do so at any time. Your agent may present the power of attorney to a bank or other third party, or your agent may be required to record your power of attorney at the parish clerk of court office, and then submit a "certified copy" to the bank or third party. If the power of attorney is effective immediately, your agent can act for you at any time until the power of attorney is revoked or terminated.

Springing Power of Attorney

Some people do not want to give anyone else the right to transact for them. However, you may want to set up what is commonly referred to as a "springing" power of attorney, which springs into effect when you become incapacitated. Your incapacity will typically be triggered when doctors certify in writing that you are unable to handle your affairs.

With a springing power of attorney, you are the only person who can transact your affairs. However, when the doctors determine that you are unable, then the person you designated as your agent in your springing power of attorney will be authorized to act for you. A springing power of attorney typically avoids the difficult court-supervised interdiction and curatorship proceeding.

Terminating Your Power of Attorney

You may terminate your power of attorney at any time. If you never terminate your power of attorney, it will be terminated by your death.

Example. Your aunt Nelda named you in her power of attorney to handle her affairs. After Nelda had a stroke, you take care of paying her bills, selling her vehicle, and buying and selling certain pieces of real estate. When Nelda dies, the power of attorney is terminated and you have no more legal authority to handle Nelda's affairs. If Nelda appointed an executor in her Will, then the executor will have the authority to handle Nelda's affairs after her death. If Nelda died without a Will, the court will likely appoint an administrator to handle Nelda's affairs after her death.

Important Provisions for Your Power of Attorney

Louisiana law in the area of power of attorney is different from all the other states. It is typically inadequate to sign a power of attorney that generally states that your agent can do "anything that you could do."

In Louisiana, you must be express about the things you want your agent to do. Express authority must be given if you want your agent to have the authority to:

- Make a donation during your lifetime, either outright or to a trust,
- Accept or reject an inheritance,
- Take out a loan,
- Sell, buy, mortgage, or lease something,
- Make health care decisions, such as surgery, medical expenses, nursing home residency, and medication.

Many improperly prepared powers of attorney do not include the express authority to make donations. When a person is incapacitated, it often becomes advantageous to a family for that person to make gifts to family members or trusts, either to avoid tax or perhaps to speed up the qualification process for Medicaid. If the power of attorney does not expressly authorize gifting, the agent does not have the authority to make these gifts.

Conclusion

Since there is good chance you will not be able to handle your own affairs at some point during your life, a properly executed power of attorney is one of the most important documents in your overall estate plan. Items to remember regarding your power of attorney include:

- You designate who can handle your affairs upon your incapacity;
- Having a power of attorney in place may avoid the burdensome court-controlled interdiction proceeding;
- Your power of attorney can be general or it can be limited to certain transactions;
- Your power of attorney can be effective immediately when signed or it can be effective only upon your disability;
- In Louisiana, certain provisions must be expressly stated in the document, such as the authority to buy, sell, donate, or make medical decisions.

Chapter 5

Louisiana Intestate Laws
What Happens When You Die without a Will?

You have probably heard stories about what happens to your assets if you live in Louisiana and you die without a Will. Maybe you have heard that your entire estate goes to the government. Maybe you have heard that probate will take 20-30% of your estate. Perhaps you have heard that your children could force your surviving spouse to sell everything so they can get their share. The purpose of this chapter is to describe what happens to your assets when you die without a Last Will and Testament.

You and Your Spouse Have Community Property

Louisiana is a community property state. In general, everything a married couple acquires during their marriage is owned one-half by each spouse, regardless of who earned it and regardless of how the asset is titled.

There are certain exceptions to the rule that everything is owned 50-50. Assets are the separate property of one spouse if that spouse inherited the asset, was the recipient of a gift, or one spouse acquired the asset before his or her marriage. However, there is a presumption in Louisiana law in favor of community property so it is important for good records to be kept if a spouse wants his or her separate property to maintain its separate property status.

Example. Bill and Mary are married. Bill inherits $50,000 from his mother. This is Bill's separate property owned only by Bill. It is not community property owned by Bill and Mary. Bill deposits these funds into the joint checking account he and Mary have had for years. Bill and Mary continue to deposit their paychecks and pay their monthly bills out of this same account. Because Bill's separate property was "commingled" with Bill and Mary's community property, all of the account will likely be deemed community property.

If, in the previous example, Bill had deposited his $50,000 inheritance into a new bank account and had kept those inherited funds apart from their community funds, then Bill could have maintained the separate status of those funds.

Remember that:

- Louisiana is a community property state which means that each spouse owns one-half of all the marital assets;
- A spouse can have separate property if he or she received an inheritance, received a gift, or acquired assets before the marriage;

- Separate property commingled with community property can cause the separate property to lose it is separate property status.

You are Married with Children and You Die without a Will

All states, including Louisiana, have laws that determine what happens to your assets if you die without a Last Will and Testament. These laws are called "intestate" laws. If you have a valid Will when you die, you will have died "testate."

Louisiana intestate laws provide that when a married person dies, his half of the community property goes to his children (the children are called naked owners), but his wife receives the usufruct of his half of the community property until she either dies or remarries.

What Is a Usufruct?

Usufruct is one of the most misunderstood terms in Louisiana estate planning law. Usufruct is a term used exclusively in Louisiana and is a very common form of ownership in Louisiana, particularly among married couples. Essentially, when a spouse inherits the usufruct of assets, the surviving spouse has the right to "use" and receive the "fruits" from the assets until the usufruct is terminated.

Example. Bill and Mary have a bank account with $60,000 of community funds. This could be a checking account, savings account, or certificate of deposit. Bill dies intestate (without a Will). Bill and Mary have three children. Mary continues to own her half of the account ($30,000). Since Bill died intestate, Mary inherits the usufruct of Bill's half of the account. Bill's three children are the naked owners of Bill's $30,000. As usufructuary, Mary becomes the owner of the entire $60,000 account, but when she dies or remarries, Bill's children (the naked owners) will have a claim against Mary's estate for the $30,000 over which she had the usufruct.

When you die intestate owning community property with your spouse, your spouse will inherit the usufruct of your share of the community property, and your children will inherit the naked ownership of your share of the community property. Yes, ownership of your assets will be divided into two parts - usufruct and naked ownership.

You Are Married and You Own Separate Property - Watch Out

Watch out if you are married and you own separate property. Many married people owning separate property want their spouse to benefit from their separate property. However, Louisiana intestate laws provide that if a married person owns separate property when he or she dies intestate, that separate property will bypass the surviving spouse and go directly to the children.

Example. Bill inherited stock in ABC, Inc. Bill and his wife, Mary, were living off the quarterly dividends from the stock. Bill died intestate (without a Will). Since the stock was Bill's separate property, it went straight to Bill's children, and Mary was deprived of that income for the rest of her life.

You Are Single and You Die without a Will

If you are not married when you die and you die
without a Will, your assets will go to your children. If
any of your children died before you, then that
predeceased child's share will go to that child's
children. If you do not have children, your assets will
go to your brothers and sisters (subject to your
parents having the usufruct if they are still alive). If
any of your brothers or sisters died before you, then
that sibling's share will go to that sibling's children.

What Is Probate and How Do the Assets Get Transferred to the Heirs?

When a Louisiana resident dies owning assets (such as
real estate, vehicles, stock, or bank accounts) titled in
his or her name, a succession must be done so the
assets can be transferred to the appropriate heirs.

When you start the process of handling a succession,
you will need to gather records that describe what the
person owned when he or she died, such as bank
statements, brokerage firm statements, stock
certificates, vehicle titles, and copies of real estate
purchases. You will take these records with you when
you meet with the attorney you have chosen to handle
the succession.
The attorney should ask you several questions and
then determine whether an "administration" is
necessary. If the succession is not complicated, an
administration is probably not necessary.
Circumstances that often require an administration
include:

- Assets need to be sold or managed prior to the completion of the succession;
- There is disagreement among the heirs;
- The deceased has bills that need to be paid promptly;
- It will take a long time to determine the assets and debts of the deceased; or
- Any other complicating factor.

If an administration is necessary, the attorney will assist the family in determining who should petition to be named as the administrator by a judge. The surviving spouse or a child is often the one to petition to be named as the administrator. The attorney will prepare a number of legal documents and then file those at the parish courthouse. If it is not contested and if all the legal requirements are met, the judge will appoint the petitioner as the administrator.

The administrator's job is to collect all the assets of the deceased. He will likely open a bank account in the name of the succession and deposit all succession funds in that bank account. The administrator cannot spend any of the succession funds without a judge's approval. There are strict rules in Louisiana regarding an administrator's rights and obligations.

Whether there is an administration or not, the attorney will prepare a number of legal documents. One of those documents is commonly called the Detailed Descriptive List. This is a detailed listing of all the assets of the deceased, as well as all the debts of the deceased and the succession. This list shows all the assets and liabilities as of the date the person died. All of the assets must show a value.

Finally, the attorney will prepare a legal document called a Judgment of Possession. This document, which will be signed by a judge, orders banks, financial institutions, and other third parties to transfer title of assets listed in the Judgment of Possession (JOP), from the name of the person who died to the names of the heirs.

Example. John died intestate on January 10 leaving two children, Phil and Susan. John owned a house, three bank accounts, stock, and a car. John had no debt. Phil gathered all the information on the assets, and he took it to the attorney to handle the succession. The attorney prepared a number of legal documents, including a Detailed Descriptive List of Assets and Liabilities. Many of these documents were signed by Phil and Susan. The attorney filed these documents at the parish courthouse and the judge later signed a Judgment of Possession (JOP) ordering that John's assets be transferred to Phil and Susan. The attorney then recorded a certified copy of this JOP in the parish real estate records - this transferred title of John's home. Phil and Susan took a copy of the JOP to the bank. The bank closed out John's accounts and wrote equal checks to Phil and Susan. Phil sent John's stock certificates to the company's transfer agent who mailed new stock certificates to Phil and Susan. Finally, Phil and Susan went to the Department of Motor Vehicles and had a new title issued to them for their dad's car.

Are Any Taxes Due When Someone Dies Intestate?

Louisiana phased out its Inheritance Tax in 2004. Congress has imposed a federal estate tax on large estates. For deaths occurring in the year 2014, the first $5,300,000 in value is exempt from the federal estate tax. The estate tax rates are about 40% of the estate that exceeds the exemption amount. When a married person dies intestate, there is often no getting around this estate tax.

Example. Bill and Mary owned $8,000,000 in community property. Bill had another $4,000,000 in separate property. Bill died intestate during 2014 when the estate tax exemption was $5,300,000. His estate equals $8,000,000 ($4,000,000 community property plus $4,000,000 separate property). His estate owes about $1,080,000 in federal estate tax to the IRS - due within nine months of Bill's death.

The big problem was that Bill died intestate. If Bill had a proper Will, there would have been no estate tax (due to a provision in our tax code that allows there to be no tax due upon the death of the first spouse to die if the Will is written correctly).

Conclusion

When a Louisiana resident dies without a Last Will and Testament:
- Louisiana intestate laws favor the children over the spouse;
- If you own community property with your spouse, your spouse will inherit the usufruct of

your half of the community property until he or she dies or remarries, and your children inherit the naked ownership;

- If you own separate property and you are married, your separate property will bypass your spouse and go directly to your children;
- If you are single when you die, your assets will go to your children, and if you do not have children, your assets will go to your brothers and sisters;
- A succession will be necessary to transfer ownership of your assets; and
- Federal estate tax may be due if you have a large estate (over $5,300,000 for death occurring during 2014).

Chapter 6

Your Last Will and Testament
Maybe the Most Important Document You Ever Sign

Your Last Will and Testament (also referred to as your "Will") may be the most important document you ever sign. You have spent your lifetime saving and investing for yourself, your family and your loved ones. Your Last Will and Testament allows you to leave your possessions behind to the people that mean the most to you.

Reasons for Writing a Will

There are a number of good reasons why you should write a Will, including but not limited to:

- Designating to whom you want your assets to go when you die;
- Designating the executor or co-executors of your estate;
- Minimizing or avoiding federal estate tax;
- Taking advantage of forced heirship laws if you want to minimize what goes to a forced heir;

- Providing for contingencies that might occur such as a spouse or a child predeceasing you;
- Making it easier for your spouse to sell assets you leave to him or her;
- Providing that your executor can serve as an independent executor, which can allow your estate to be settled more quickly and without significant court supervision;
- Establishing testamentary trusts for the benefit of those heirs who might need help managing their inheritance.

What Makes a Will Valid in Louisiana

For a Will to be valid, it must be made in a form that is expressly authorized by Louisiana law. In Louisiana, there are two forms of Wills: olographic and notarial.

Olographic Will

An olographic Will is a document entirely written, dated, and signed in your handwriting. Your olographic Will must be signed at the end of the Will. The olographic Will is subject to no other requirement as to form. It does not need to be witnessed or notarized to be valid.

While olographic Wills are valid, they are not recommended. Lay people typically do not have the expertise to properly draft a Will. While it is easy to create an olographic Will that is considered valid, it is difficult to draft a Will that covers everything that needs to be covered with clarity. The improper inclusion or exclusion of one word can cause ambiguity which often leads heirs to argue. Considering its importance, it is widely believed that you should hire an attorney to prepare your Will. This ensures use of the proper legal language to document your intentions.

Notarial Will

As opposed to the olographic Will which is entirely in your own handwriting, the notarial Will is typed. You will sign your notarial Will at the end and on each separate page. A notary and two witnesses will sign a declaration similar to the following: "In our presence the testator has declared or signified that this instrument is his Last Will and Testament and has signed it at the end and on each other separate page, and in the presence of the testator and each other we have hereunto subscribed our names this __ day of _____ 201_."

There are additional requirements for a notarial Will if:

- You know how to sign your name and read, but you are unable to sign your name because of a physical infirmity;
- You do not know how to read, or you are physically impaired to the extent that you cannot read, whether or not you are able to sign your name;
- You are blind but physically able to read Braille; or
- You have been legally declared deaf or deaf and blind and you are able to read sign language, Braille, or visual English.

Estate Planning in Louisiana

Important Provisions to Include in Your Will

The meat of the Last Will and Testament is typically in the bequests (also called "dispositions"). In Louisiana, bequests in Wills are classified as particular, general, or universal.

A universal bequest (or legacy) is a bequest of all of your estate, or the balance of the estate that remains after particular legacies are satisfied.

A general legacy is one in which you bequeath a fraction or a certain proportion of the estate, or a fraction or certain proportion of the balance of the estate that remains after particular legacies are satisfied.

An example of a particular legacy of cash is as follows: "I leave to my nephew, Austin H. Johnson, the sum of twenty-five thousand dollars ($25,000), cash, in full ownership."

Another example of a particular legacy is a bequest of real estate. Example: "I leave to my son, Jack Jones, Jr., all of my interest in the property located at 123 Florida Boulevard, Baton Rouge, Louisiana." It generally is not necessary to list the complete legal description of the property when including a bequest of real estate in your Will.

Sometimes people make bequests of corporate stock in their Will. Example: "I leave 1,000 shares of ExxonMobil common stock to my grandson, Tim Jones." You may also want to make a provision in this bequest so that if the stock splits or if the capital structure of ExxonMobil changes (such as if they are merged into another company), then this bequest would include those additional shares acquired through the stock split, merger, or acquisition.

Many of the Wills we prepare do not include any bequests of particular assets. For example, a husband's Will may provide, in general, that he leaves the usufruct of everything he owns at the time of his death to his wife for her lifetime, and he names his children as the naked owners. If you are not married, your Will may provide simply that all of your assets at the time of your death are to be divided equally among your children, without listing the specifics of any of the assets you currently own.

Naming Your Executor

Besides providing for the proper bequests, naming your executor may be the most important provision in your Will. It is your executor's job to gather all the information on the assets that you own at the time of your death, hire an attorney, make decisions regarding the sale of your assets (such as your home, vehicles, stock and other assets), pay estate debts and oversee the distribution of assets to the heirs.

The executor must comply with all the Louisiana laws that pertain to him. Penalties and personal liability can result from an executor failing to perform within the required laws. A good executor can provide for an orderly disposition of assets, while a poor executor can cause your estate to drag on for months or years unnecessarily.

Who should you name as your executor? That is a good question. It should be someone you trust and someone who is organized, fair, and trustworthy. If you are married, you may want to name your spouse as your executor and one of your adult children as your alternate executor.

If you do not have a spouse or adult child who would make an appropriate executor, you can name a trusted friend or other relative to serve as your executor. You could also name a corporate trust department, CPA, attorney, or other trusted advisor as your executor. You can also name two or more people to serve as co-executors. If you have two children, you could name them as co-executors. Many parents do this because they do not want to hurt a child's feelings by leaving them out. Do not name co-executors unless you feel they can work well together.

Allow Your Executor to Be "Independent"

It is important to provide that your executor (or co-executors) may serve as an "independent" executor. If in your Will, you state that your executor may serve as an independent executor, it will be easier for your executor to settle your estate because an independent executor does not need to constantly seek court approval to act like an executor who is not an "independent" executor.

Example. In Ralph's Will, he stated that his daughter, Heidi, could serve as independent executor. After Ralph died, it was necessary for Heidi to sell Ralph's two vehicles, his boat, his trailer, and other assets. Since she was named independent executor, she did not need to seek and obtain court approval for each sale. When she found a buyer for these items, she could sell them immediately. If she was not named as an "independent" executor, she would have needed to retain her succession attorney to petition the court to sell these items each time she wanted to sell something, incurring additional delay and expense.

Using Trusts in Your Will

Many people include trusts in their Wills. These trusts are commonly referred to as "testamentary trusts," because the trust is included in your last will and "testament."

While there are many uses for testamentary trusts, two of the most common include (1) providing for the management of your assets for your heirs after your death; and (2) married couples using trusts in their Wills to avoid federal estate tax.

Using Testamentary Trusts to Manage Assets

Let's say you want to leave your assets to your children but they are not yet mature or responsible enough to handle a lump sum of money properly (some people are never that mature or responsible). You and your spouse have two children, ages 19 and 16. You and your spouse have accumulated assets totaling $800,000 in value. You do not think that your children are capable of handling $400,000 prudently. So in your Will, you provide that the children's inheritance, if they are younger than age 30 (or whatever age you choose) at the time of your death, will be placed in trust. You will name a trustee of the trust, and you will give that trustee certain powers, such as the power to buy and sell trust assets and the power to distribute assets to your children for their health, education, maintenance, and support, prior to the termination of the trust.

Using a Testamentary Trust to Avoid Estate Tax

Married couples often include testamentary trusts in their Wills to help avoid estate tax. The estate tax exemption for the year 2014 is $5,300,000 so far fewer families are subject to this tax than before when the estate tax exemption was $600,000.

Nonetheless a married person can leave his or her estate in trust, name the surviving spouse as the income beneficiary of that trust, and follow other requirements, and there will be no federal estate tax required to be paid at the death of the first spouse to die. This trust is commonly referred to as a bypass trust or a QTIP trust. This estate tax avoidance technique can also be accomplished by leaving your spouse the usufruct of your assets for the rest of your spouse's lifetime.

Other Common Provisions in Wills

Survivorship provision. Many people ask, "What if I leave an inheritance to someone and that person dies right after me?" Well, you can include a survivorship provision in your Will so you can control where the inheritance goes if your legatee dies right after you. You can provide in your Will that the bequests in your Will are not effective unless the legatee survives you for a certain period (six months is the maximum period of time allowed).

Collation. Sometimes a parent with more than one child will, during his or her lifetime, financially help one child more than the other. The parent may feel that it is fair to reduce the inheritance of that particular child who received gifts during the parent's lifetime. The parent may provide in his or her Will that certain gifts made to children will be subject to collation so that those gifts made to those children will be counted as an advance on their inheritance.

Provisions Not to Include in Wills

There are certain things related to planning for death that should not be listed in the Last Will and Testament. Your Will may not be read until days or even weeks after your death when it is too late to abide by your wishes. The following are examples of items that should not be listed in your Will.

Organ Donation. If you wish to be an organ donor, you should do so by filling out and signing the necessary information provided by the Louisiana Organ Procurement Agency at www.lopa.org, as well as documenting that you are an organ donor on the back of your Louisiana Driver's License. Every year our law firm is the major sponsor of the Rabalais Run For Life, a 5k Run/Half Mile Walk that raises tens of thousands of dollars each year to support organ donation awareness in Louisiana.

Decisions Regarding Life Support Machines. Your living will is the proper place to document your decision regarding life support machines, not your Last Will and Testament.

Beneficiary Designation Items. Individual retirement accounts, 401(k) plans, life insurance and annuities are transferred to the persons designated on your beneficiary designation form held by the financial institution or insurance company. Do not make a bequest of an IRA in your Will.

Example. Don has an IRA worth $250,000. In his Will, he stated that he wanted his IRA to go to his son, Jason. However, when Don opened his IRA account, he named his daughter, Emily, as the beneficiary of his IRA. After Don dies, the financial institution will deliver the IRA funds to Emily even though Don stated in his Will that he wanted those funds to go to Jason.

Personal Effects. The proper disposition of personal effects can be tricky. It is simple to divide a $100,000 bank account among four children (each child gets $25,000). It is not so simple to divide up your jewelry, china, furniture, tools, guns, family photos, and other personal effects among multiple heirs. There are two ways to provide for the disposition of your personal effects - in your Will or outside of your Will.

Disposing of Your Personal Effects in Your Will

One way to dispose of your personal effects is to make bequests of these items in your Will. You might say something like, "I leave my diamond engagement ring to my daughter, Jenny." Or you might say, "I leave all of my tools to my son, Jason."

Disposing of your personal effects in your Will can be burdensome. You have to list all of these items in your Will, and you have to list who you want to inherit these items. If you change your mind or if you acquire additional items that you would like to bequeath, you have to change your Will.

However, if you think there is a chance that your heirs may fight over your personal belongings, then it may be best if you bequeath them in your Will, particularly if they have significant fair market value or significant sentimental value to your heirs.

Disposing of Personal Effects outside of Your Will

Some people will attempt to dispose of their personal effects outside of their Will. They might place a sticky note on each item that states who gets each item, or they may make a separate list in their own handwriting and change it from time to time, or they may simply ask their children to work it out, or take turns picking items. There is no limit on the number of ways personal items can be passed along to your loved ones. This informal method can work well, particularly if your heirs get along well and can agree on an orderly disposition of these items.

Whichever way you choose to dispose of your personal items, it is important to communicate your desires rather than leave it up to your heirs to make all the decisions.

Conclusion

When you prepare your Will, it is important to keep these things in mind:

- There are two forms of valid Wills in Louisiana: olographic and notarial. Most Wills are notarial;
- Properly describing your bequests may be the most important part of your Will;
- Choosing your independent executor is also an important decision to document properly;
- It may be helpful to include a testamentary trust in your Will;
- Other important provisions to include in your Will are survivorship provisions, contingent bequests, and whether you want lifetime gifts collated;
- There are certain provisions that should not be in your Will.

Chapter 7

Protect Your Children and Grandchildren

How to Preserve Your Assets from Taxes, Long-Term Care Costs, and Your Children's Divorces and Poor Spending Habits

M any people engage in estate planning to protect their estates for their children and grandchildren. The failure to properly plan your estate could result in any of the following:

- The wrong people raise your children if you die before your children reach the age of majority;
- Your heirs blow their inheritance, because they were not mature enough to handle it properly;
- Your children have to split their inheritance with their spouse when your children get divorced;
- Your loved ones have to make difficult medical decisions for you – like the removal of life support systems – with no previous guidance from you;

- Your children have to go to court to fight others to get legal authority to manage your affairs when you become incapacitated;
- Your executor must pay considerable federal estate tax within nine months after your death;
- Your executor has to post a bond to become the executor of your estate and they have to get a judge's permission to sell your home, car, or other assets after you die.

Proper estate planning can avoid most, if not all, of these problems for your children or grandchildren (or anyone else you intend to benefit with estate planning).

Guardians for Minor Children

Parents with children under the age of eighteen need to write their Will so they can designate who will raise the children if the parents die before their children reach the age of majority (which is age 18 in Louisiana).

In Louisiana, you can designate who you want to be your children's "tutor" if you and the other parent die before the child reaches the age of 18. The last surviving parent has the right to designate who will be the minor child's tutor. The failure to designate the tutor for your children will result in a judge designating a tutor. Your choice for who can best raise your child or children may be different than a judge's choice.

Paul A. Rabalais

Creating a Testamentary Trust for Young Children

If your children are young, or if they are not yet mature enough to handle a lump sum inheritance, you should designate in your Will that when you die, your assets will be placed in trust. This helps ensure that your child's inheritance will be managed by the right person and used for the right reasons. A testamentary trust for minor children will also avoid the expensive and difficult tutorship proceeding that applies when a minor inherits property.

Example. Mark and Colleen have two minor children. Mark dies unexpectedly. Colleen decides to sell their home. However, since Mark did not have a Will which should have included a testamentary trust for their two children, Colleen was unable to sell their home right away. She first had to pay thousands of dollars in attorney fees and court costs to get herself confirmed as the tutor of Mark's children and get court permission to sell the children's interest in their father's home.

If Mark, in the previous example, had written a Will which had included a testamentary trust for his children naming Colleen as trustee, then Colleen would have been able to sell the home shortly after Mark's death without having to spend a fortune on the difficult tutorship proceeding. Mark's half of the home would have been re-titled in Colleen's name as trustee of Mark's children's trust, and Colleen would have been permitted to sell the home without having to get court approval to do so.

Forced Heirship

Louisiana is the only state that has forced heirship. However, forced heirship laws have changed over the years.

In the past, all children were forced heirs and could not be excluded from receiving part of their parent's estate. Now, forced heirs are defined, in general, as children 23 years of age or younger, or children of any age that are permanently incapable of administering their own estate.

Example. Steve dies survived by a wife and three children ages 28, 25 and 20. Steve bequeathed his entire estate to his wife in his Last Will and Testament. Steve's 20 year old child is a forced heir and has a right to claim a portion of his father's assets.

If a person dies with one forced heir, that forced heir is entitled to one-fourth of the deceased's estate. If a person dies with two or more forced heirs, then those forced heirs are entitled to divide one-half of the deceased's estate.

Prevent Your Children and Grandchildren from Wasting Their Inheritance

An inheritance is typically not earned. Children and grandchildren often look at an inheritance as a freebie. You often read about lottery winners squandering away their winnings; people who receive an inheritance are no different. Since they did not work for or earn their inheritance, they do not value the money as much as you may value it.

Example. Leonard and Jackie worked all of their lives to build their estate of $600,000. They clipped coupons, bought items that were on sale, and avoided travel, eating out and other luxuries because they said these things were "too expensive." When Leonard and Jackie died, their two children each inherited $300,000. Their son, Billy, immediately purchased a new boat, a new truck, and many other items that years later had no value.

Leonard and Jackie could have arranged their Wills so that upon their deaths, their assets would have been transferred to a trust. Leonard and Jackie could have named a trustee (either an individual or a corporate trustee) to manage the assets for their children. The trust might say that the children receive all the income from the trust assets, and the trustee can give the principal to the children for their health, education, maintenance, or support. Perhaps the trust would also provide that the children would receive one-half of the trust assets when they reach the age of forty, and the rest when they reach the age of fifty.

This type of trust is called a testamentary trust. The terms of the trust are in your Last Will and Testament, and the trust owns no assets until you die. There are many different ways to set up a testamentary trust, but the most important decisions are:

- Who will be the trustee? You can have one trustee or multiple co-trustees. The trustee can be an individual or a corporate trustee such as a bank trust department.

- When can trust principal be used? You can provide that trust principal can be used for education only, or you can broaden it to say that principal can also be used for the health or general welfare of the beneficiary. There are few restrictions.
- How long will the trust last? You can provide that the beneficiaries will receive the trust principal at a certain age (such as 25), or you can give the trustee discretion regarding when the beneficiary will receive the trust assets.

Protect Your Children from Their Divorces

The divorce rate is higher now than it was 30 or 40 years ago. While it is uncommon for a couple that has been married for 40+ years to get divorced, it is common for one or more of their children to get divorced.

By definition, an inheritance that your child receives is his or her separate property. However, your child's inheritance will quickly become community property co-owned with your son-in-law or daughter-in-law unless it is handled properly. If your son or daughter gets divorced after receiving their inheritance, he or she may be required to split their inheritance with his or her ex-spouse.

Example. Jason received an inheritance of $400,000 from his parents. His parents saved all of their lives so Jason could benefit from the inheritance. This inheritance initially is Jason's separate property. Jason invests the money, and these investments produce interest and dividends. The interest and dividends from Jason's separate property are community property owned equally by Jason and his wife. The community property and separate property get mixed up together so no one can accurately determine what is separate property and what is community property. When this happens, it all becomes community property due to the presumption in Louisiana law which provides that all assets in the name of either spouse are community property.

One way to protect your children from having to split their inheritance when they divorce is to provide that the inheritance for each child of yours will be put in trust. This will make it more likely that the inherited assets will not be commingled with community property that your child owns with his or her spouse.

Another way your children can protect their inheritance from divorce is to sign a document whereby they declare that all income from their separate property is their separate property. This document will need to be recorded in the parish records to be effective, but it will keep income from separate property from being classified as community property.

Using Powers of Attorney

One of the best legal strategies you can employ for your children is to sign a power of attorney that makes it easier for one or more of your children (or some other person you designate) to handle your affairs for you if you are unable to handle your own affairs. Simply executing a properly prepared power of attorney may prevent your children from having to go through the burdensome interdiction proceeding often required when someone become incapacitated without previously executing a power of attorney.

Example. George is widowed with three children. George owns an IRA from which he takes periodic distributions when he needs living expenses. George suddenly has a stroke that renders him unable to sign his name or understand that he needs funds to live on. Since George did not previously execute a power of attorney, one or more of his children will be forced to hire attorneys to sue their father, have him declared legally incompetent, and obtain the authority to act for him. In Louisiana, this proceeding can take months or years and cost thousands of dollars. If George had previously executed a power of attorney, the person of George's choosing would be able to continue to manage George's assets for him just as if George were doing it for himself.

If you are married, you are likely to designate your spouse as the first person to have authority to act for you on your power of attorney, and you may designate an adult child or children as the alternate if your spouse is unable to act for you.

Sign a Living Will Declaration

The Terry Schiavo matter in Florida brought a great deal of attention to living wills. You can designate in a living will (also known as a "Declaration") your intentions regarding the withdrawal or withholding of life support machines if you are in a profound comatose state with no reasonable chance of recovery.

By signing a living will, you will be making your own decision regarding life support machines and making that decision known to your family and your doctors.

Children of elderly parents often have a sense of relief when their parent on life support machines has previously signed a living will. The children do not want to make that final decision for their parent to withdraw life support machines, and it is easier for family members when the patient has previously executed a living will stating his or her intentions regarding life support machines.

Preserving Your Assets from the Cost of Long-term Care

Example. Ernest and Elizabeth have accumulated assets totaling $300,000 during their lives. They discover that if they have to move to a nursing home because they need assistance with their daily living activities due to an illness such as severe arthritis or Alzheimer's disease, it will cost each of them about $6,000 per month to live in the nursing home. They realize that paying for nursing home costs for two to three years will deplete their life savings.

You have a few options regarding the payment of your long-term care expenses:

1. You can pay for them yourself until you run out of money and then hopefully you will qualify for Medicaid, which will pay your nursing home expenses;
2. You can purchase long-term care insurance which will pay for some or all of the cost of your

care. Many senior citizens either do not want to purchase long-term care insurance because they feel it is too expensive, or they cannot purchase it because they do not pass the medical underwriting tests required by the insurance company; or

3. You can carefully engage in Medicaid planning which often involves transferring ownership of certain assets to other family members or certain trusts.

Whichever method you choose, make certain you fully understand your options before you act. Making the wrong move can be worse than not acting at all.

Minimizing Taxes

You can help your children or other heirs by planning your estate so that federal estate taxes, capital gains taxes, and income taxes are minimized.

The federal estate tax exemption increased to $5,300,000 on January 1, 2014. This increase in the exemption will preclude many estates from having to pay federal estate tax. If you have an estate exceeding $5,300,000, there may be estate tax planning techniques available to you, such as annual exclusion gifts, transfers to a spouse, or charitable giving techniques that can reduce the amount of federal estate tax your estate will be required to pay.

Under current tax law, the capital gains tax basis of your assets will be "stepped-up" when you die.

Example. Over the years, Rod purchased IBM stock. He paid a total of $60,000 for the stock. At his death, the stock Rod had purchased had a fair market value of $260,000. Had Rod sold the stock just before his death, there would have been $200,000 of taxable capital gain. However, Rod did not sell the stock. When he died and left the stock to his children, the children inherit the stock with a new stepped-up basis of $260,000. If the children sell the stock for $260,000, there will be no capital gain and thus no capital gains tax.

If, however, you give appreciated assets to your children during your lifetime, they will receive a "carry-over" basis. If Rod had given the stock to his children before he died, their basis would have been $60,000, and there would be considerable capital gains tax due on their sale of the stock for $260,000.

You can help your children minimize income taxes as well. If your IRA beneficiary designations are set up properly, your children can elect to take taxable distributions over their lifetime, minimizing the income tax they will have to pay in the years immediately after your death.

Allow Executor to Serve as Independent Executor

Laws were recently passed in Louisiana authorizing a simpler form of probate in Louisiana. Under the old system, your executor would have to get court approval after your death to pay the estate's debts or to sell the estate's assets. This is time-consuming and complicated.

Now, if in your Will you have authorized your executor to act as an "independent executor," once your executor is confirmed by a judge, they will be able to sell succession assets and pay succession debts without having to go back to court to get approval from a judge to do so. You can make matters easier for your children or executor if you have designated in your Will that your executor may serve under this easier "independent administration" procedure.

Conclusion

You can protect your children and grandchildren by:

- Naming guardians in your Will for your minor children so the person you choose can raise your children;
- Bequeathing your estate in trust for your children so they can benefit from their inheritance for the rest of their lifetime;
- Making your children's inheritance divorce-proof;
- Complying with Louisiana's forced heirship laws;
- Signing a power of attorney and living will so your children will not be burdened with difficult decisions upon your disability;
- Preserving your assets from the cost of long-term care;
- Minimizing or avoiding federal estate tax.

Chapter 8

Multiple Marriages
Protect Your Second Spouse AND Your Children from Your First Spouse

The Louisiana community property laws work well for most traditional Louisiana families, where the husband and wife have children together. After both the husband and wife die, their combined assets are typically divided equally among their children. It can be pretty straightforward.

We now live in a society where it is "normal" for people to get married two or more times. It is not uncommon, and often encouraged, for surviving spouses to remarry after the death of their first spouse. Many people get a divorce and then marry someone else.

Proper estate planning is critical in multiple marriage situations – particularly when each spouse has children from a prior marriage.

Typical Example That Excludes the Children

Larry and Martha get married at age 60. They each have two adult children from their prior marriages. Larry wants to provide for both his new wife and his two children. He writes a Will leaving everything he owns to his wife. He also stipulates that if Martha dies before him, he wants everything he owns to go to his two children when he dies. Larry dies and all of his assets go to Martha. When Martha dies five years later, she leaves everything she owns to her two children. Larry's two children get nothing.

Common Example excluding the Spouse

Steve and Dot get married at age 60. Steve brings into the marriage assets worth $1,000,000, including the home Steve and Dot live in. Dot's assets are less than $100,000. Steve has three children from his prior marriage. Steve wants to provide for Dot and his three children when he dies, but he does not get his affairs in order. When Steve dies unexpectedly, all of Steve's assets, including the home and other assets Steve brought into the marriage (these assets are his separate property, because he brought them into the marriage) are transferred to Steve's three children under the intestate laws, and Dot must move out of the home. Dot will have no financial support for the rest of her lifetime.

Much of the bickering that takes place over an inheritance occurs when children and their step-parent fight over a deceased's assets. The relationship that a child has with his or her step-parent, in general, is often not as strong as the relationship a child has with his or her surviving parent.

Paul A. Rabalais

Community Property Rules Confuse Uninformed

Married people often mistakenly believe that if they each keep their accounts in their own name, they will avoid problems upon a death or divorce because they each have their own accounts. Louisiana community property laws, however, do not work that way.

The following is an example of what can, and does, go wrong when couples do not plan properly:

1. When Dan gets married to Jackie, he has accounts totaling $500,000 in his name only. At the moment he gets married, those accounts are Dan's separate property because he owned them prior to his marriage.
2. During Dan's marriage, his accounts produce $175,000 of interest and dividends, which get added to his accounts. These "fruits" are community property even though they are in Dan's name only.
3. Dan worked during the marriage and he deposited $150,000 of his wages into his accounts. Wages are community property even though they are the result of Dan's efforts and are deposited into Dan's accounts.
4. Dan and Jackie spent some of the money in Dan's accounts during their marriage on travel and other expenses. When Dan died, there was $400,000 in Dan's accounts, consisting of cash and certificates of deposit. Dan died without a Will, but he was not concerned about the lack of a Will because of Louisiana's intestate laws that provide that Dan's separate property goes to his children when he dies. Dan and his children

both understood that Dan wanted these accounts to go to his children when he died.

5. Were Dan's accounts his separate property when he died? Not likely. There is a presumption of community property in Louisiana, and when community property (such as fruits and wages) get mixed with separate property (assets brought into the marriage), it may be determined that all the funds have become community property.

6. If Dan's accounts total $400,000, and he died intestate and the accounts are community property, Jackie owns $200,000 (as her half of the community) and Jackie gets the usufruct of Dan's $200,000 until Jackie dies or remarries. At that point, Jackie, or her estate, will owe Dan's children $200,000.

Community Property Rules

It is important for married couples and their adult children to understand how Louisiana community property laws apply. Proper planning and education can eliminate unnecessary bickering that often occurs upon the death of a person who had children from a prior marriage.

Definitions

Community property rules apply to all married couples in the state of Louisiana. Everything that married people own is either community property or separate property.

Community Property

Each spouse owns a one-half interest in the community property. Things in the possession of a spouse during the existence of a marriage are presumed to be community property, but it may be proven that things are separate property. Community property consists of:

- Property acquired during the existence of the marriage through the effort or skill of either spouse;
- Property acquired with community property;
- Property donated to spouses jointly;
- Damages awarded for loss or injury to community property; and
- All other property not classified as separate property.

Common forms of community property include the wages of a spouse, a business started during the marriage by one or both spouses, and any assets purchased with community funds.

Separate Property

The separate property of a spouse is his or hers exclusively. Separate property includes:

- Property acquired by a spouse prior to the marriage;
- Property acquired by a spouse with separate things;

- Property acquired by a spouse by inheritance or a donation to him or her individually; and
- Damages awarded to a spouse resulting from fraud or bad faith of the other spouse.

Common forms of separate property include things acquired by a spouse prior to the marriage, an inheritance by a spouse, and a gift to one spouse.

Reservation of Fruits as Separate Property

Income derived from the separate property of a spouse is community property. However, a spouse may reserve this income as his or her separate property by signing a certain type of declaration that meets the requirements of Louisiana law and is recorded in the conveyance records of the proper parish.

Example. Stan and Linda are married. Stan inherited 10,000 shares of ABC, Inc., stock. The stock produces a quarterly dividend of $5,000 payable to Stan. This dividend is community property owned by Stan and Linda unless Stan signs the appropriate declaration and has it recorded in the parish where he is domiciled. After the declaration is recorded, the future dividends will be Stan's separate property.

Marriage Contract

Many married couples, especially those married couples who enter marriage with children from a previous marriage, sign a marriage contract, also known as a pre-nup, pre-nuptial agreement, separate property agreement, or matrimonial agreement. These agreements typically are used to allow married couples to deviate from the traditional community property rules and often to provide that no community property will exist between the spouses and that all assets will be the separate property of either the husband or the wife.

Example. George and Jane are getting married. George has three children from his first marriage. Jane has two children. They sign a marriage contract which provides that they will have separate property only. During the marriage, George has income both from his employment and his investments. All of these earnings and assets continue to be George's separate property. When George dies, he leaves all of these assets to his three children. Jane does not own any part of these assets as community property.

If spouses enter into marriage contracts, they typically do it before their marriage. Married couples may only enter into these marriage contracts after marriage with court approval. However, if a married couple has signed a marriage contract and they want to terminate it and subject themselves to the community property rules, they may do so at any time without court approval.

Married Couples Moving to Louisiana

During the first year after moving to Louisiana, spouses may enter into a marriage contract without court approval.

Estate Planning in Louisiana

Last Will and Testament

Big mistakes are often made when married persons, particularly those who have children from a previous marriage, leave all of their assets to their current spouse in their Will.

Example. Jude and Laura are each married for the second time. They each have two children from their prior marriages. Jude wants to provide for his new wife, so he signs a Will leaving all of his property to Laura. He trusts that Laura will leave a substantial bequest to Jude's children. When Jude dies, all of his assets are put in Laura's name. Jude's adult children get nothing. Laura's Will now provides that everything she owns when she dies goes to Laura's two children. When Laura dies, Jude's children get nothing.

There are basically three ways a married person can protect his children from a previous marriage:

1. Leave bequests to your children directly, even if you die before your spouse;
2. Leave your spouse the usufruct of your property and name your children as the naked owners; and
3. Leave your assets in trust for the benefit of your spouse and your children.

Bequests to Children Directly

Even if you are married, you can bequeath assets directly to your children if you want to make sure they inherit from you.

Example. Dan and Carol are married. They are each in their second marriage, and they are each 70 years old. Dan has two condos and stock that he wants his children to inherit. Dan provides in his Last Will and Testament that he wants his four children to inherit these condos and this stock. When he dies, these assets get transferred directly to his four children.

Marital Portion

If in the previous example Dan had died "rich" in comparison with his wife, Carol, under Louisiana law, Carol would have been entitled to claim the marital portion from Dan's succession. The idea is to prevent a spouse from being left in poverty on the death of the other after having become accustomed to the wealth of the deceased.

The marital portion is one-fourth of the deceased's assets if the deceased died without children, the same fraction in usufruct for life if the deceased is survived by three or fewer children, and the marital portion is a child's share in usufruct if the deceased is survived by more than three children. In no event, however, can the marital portion exceed one million dollars.

Example. Rich dies leaving his entire $2,000,000 estate to his two children. Rich's wife, Nancy, has an estate of $50,000 at the time of Rich's death. Nancy may claim a marital portion of $500,000 from Rich's estate. Since Rich had two children, Nancy will receive the lifetime usufruct of assets totaling $500,000 in value from Rich's estate. Rich's children will receive the other $1,500,000 from Rich's estate, and they will receive the assets over which Nancy has a usufruct when she dies or when her usufruct is terminated.

Bequeath Usufruct to Your Spouse and Naked Ownership to Your Children

If you are married and you have children from a previous spouse, you may want to leave your spouse the usufruct of your assets, and leave your children the naked ownership. This can protect both your spouse and your children.

Example. Rob is married to Dot. Rob has four children from his first marriage. Rob owns a home, stock, and $200,000 of cash and bank accounts. In Rob's Will, he leaves Dot the usufruct of his assets until she dies or remarries, and he leaves his four children the naked ownership of his assets. When Rob dies, Dot can continue to live in Rob's home, she will receive the dividends from Rob's stock, and when she dies or remarries, she will owe Rob's four children a total of $200,000.

Rob must be careful when structuring his Will. If he wants to make things easy for Dot, he will provide that she can have the usufruct without posting a bond, and he will provide that she will have the authority to sell assets over which she has the usufruct without having to get the permission of Rob's children. However, there is always the chance that Dot could waste or squander the assets and nothing would be left when Dot's usufruct terminates for Rob's children.

If Rob does not waive the bond requirement, and if Rob does not give her authority to sell, then Dot will not be able to sell the stock or the home without the children's permission, and Rob's children can force Dot (since Dot is not the mother of Rob's children) to post a bond so that their inheritance is protected.

Bequeath Assets In Trust for Your Spouse and Children

If you want to provide for your spouse and your children, particularly when your spouse is not the parent of your children, you may want to structure your Will so that assets are left in trust for them after your death.

Example. Instead of leaving Dot the usufruct of his home, stock, and cash, Rob leaves them in trust for Dot and his four children. He names Dot as the income beneficiary of the trust for the rest of her lifetime, he names his four children as equal principal beneficiaries of the trust, and Rob names his son, Jimmy, as the trustee of the trust. When Rob dies, all of his assets are re-titled into the name of Jimmy as trustee of the trust. Jimmy must see to it that all of the income such as dividends and interest are paid to Dot, and he is authorized to distribute to Dot enough principal to pay for her health, education, maintenance, and support. When Dot dies, the remaining trust assets are divided among Rob's four children.

Allowing Dot to use the principal of the trust prevents her from having to reimburse Rob's children for the principal that she uses. On the other hand, if Dot has the usufruct of $200,000 of cash, and she spends

$75,000 of it after Rob dies, she will still owe Rob's children $200,000 at the termination of the usufruct.

Beneficiary Designations

If you have assets in an Individual Retirement Account (IRA) or a 401(k), or if you own life insurance or an annuity, you need to make certain that the beneficiary designations are set up properly – especially if you are married and you have children from a prior marriage.

Example. Joe retired from the local chemical plant after 30 years of employment. When he retired, he rolled his 401(k) into an IRA. In his Will, he left the usufruct of all of his assets to his second wife, Elaine, and he named his two children from his first marriage as the naked owners. Joe wanted to provide for both his current wife and his children. However, he named Elaine as the beneficiary of his IRA. His IRA, valued at $600,000 was his largest asset in value. When he died, his entire IRA went to Elaine. Elaine then rolled the IRA into an IRA in her name only and named her three children as the beneficiaries to receive the IRA at her death. When Elaine died, her children (not Joe's children) received the entire IRA.

To protect both his wife and children, Joe could have done one of two things with the beneficiary designation of his IRA:

1. Designate his wife as beneficiary of part of his IRA (let's say 50%) and designate his children as beneficiaries of the other 50%. Some financial institutions require that your spouse consent in writing when you name someone other than

your spouse as the primary beneficiary of your
IRA; or
2. Designate a trust as the beneficiary of your IRA,
so your spouse can benefit from the trust while
he or she is alive, but at your surviving spouse's
death, the trust assets (the IRA) go to your
children (and not to whomever your spouse may
designate).

Conclusion

If you or your spouse has been married more than
once:

- Avoid the trap of your separate property turning
into community property;
- Consider a marriage contract prior to your
marriage;
- Take advantage of the Louisiana usufruct or
trusts to provide for your spouse and your
children;
- Use caution when designating beneficiaries of
retirement plans, life insurance, and annuities.

Chapter 9

Death and Taxes
Benjamin Franklin Said It Best

Everyone wants to avoid tax. When many people think about avoiding taxes, they think about avoiding income tax. Louisiana residents have to be concerned with several types of taxes when they are planning their estates. Some of the taxes that can be minimized include the Louisiana Inheritance Tax, the Federal estate tax, the Louisiana Gift Tax, the income tax, the capital gains tax, and the property tax.

The Louisiana Inheritance Tax Is Gone

For many years, heirs owed the State of Louisiana an inheritance tax based on the value of their inheritance. The inheritance tax rate ranged from 2% to 10%, based on the value of the inheritance and the relationship between the deceased and the heir.

The Louisiana Inheritance Tax, generally speaking, is dead and gone. Effective January 1, 2008, the Louisiana Inheritance Tax does not apply when the death occurred after June 30, 2004.

Estate Planning in Louisiana

Federal Estate Tax

The federal estate tax applies to the estates of people who were residents in any of the 50 states when they died. When it applies, it is significant. Essentially, when a person dies, we have to add up the fair market value (as determined by appraisal or otherwise) of everything the deceased owned – their house, cars, bank accounts, IRAs, 401(k)s, life insurance, stock, businesses they own, other real estate, and much more. If the value of those assets exceeds an exemption amount ($5,300,000 for deaths occurring in 2014) there may be federal estate tax due on the amount in excess of the exemption. The taxed portion will be taxed at a rate of about 40%.

For many years the estate tax exemption was $600,000 and many more estates were subject to the federal estate tax. As the exemption has increased to $5,300,000, it has decreased the number of families and estates subject to the tax.

Future of the Estate Tax

In December 2010, sweeping new federal estate tax laws were passed. However, the new tax laws that were passed at that time were only put into effect until December 31, 2012. Since Congress and the President passed new tax laws in January, 2013, the exemption amount is $5,300,000 for deaths occurring in 2014, and the estate tax rate is 40%.

Paul A. Rabalais

Using Deceased Spouse's Unused Exclusion Amount

Under pre-2010 federal estate tax law, each spouse had an estate tax exemption. If the estate of the first spouse to die did not use his or her exemption, it would be lost and the surviving spouse could not use any of the exemption of the first spouse to die. This all changed in 2011, and the new tax act that was passed in January 2013 kept portability in place

Now we have something called "portability." It allows the surviving spouse to increase his or her exemption amount by the amount of the unused exemption amount of the deceased spouse who died after 2010.

Example. Dad died in 2014 with an estate of $2,000,000. His estate was not large enough to fully utilize the $5,300,000 exemption. Assuming an election was made by the Dad's executor, Mom's estate tax exemption will be $8.6 million ($5.3 million plus the $3.3 million that Dad's estate did not use).

Note that in order for the surviving spouse to increase his or her exemption amount, the executor of the deceased spouse's estate must make an election on the first spouse's timely-filed estate tax return.

Calculating Federal Estate Tax

Essentially, when a person dies, the executor is responsible for determining the total value of the assets the deceased owned on the date of his or her death. If the gross value of the assets exceeds the exemption amount, a federal estate tax return must be filed by the executor within nine months after the death.

The estate tax return is complicated to most people. If the deceased owned a business, a home, or other real estate, appraisals must be obtained and attached to the return.

All investments and financial accounts must be reviewed to determine date of death values, and those values must be listed on the return.

The estate is entitled to deduct certain items before calculating the net estate. Common deductions include debts the deceased owed on the date of death, costs to administer the estate, bequests to a surviving spouse, and bequests to charitable organizations.

Example. Ralph died on January 15, 2011. He and his wife Theresa together owned a home worth $1,500,000, an investment account valued at $6,500,000, an office condominium worth $2,000,000, and miscellaneous other assets such as vehicles and bank accounts totaling $500,000. The total value of their community property was $10,500,000. Ralph's half of the community property was $5,250,000. Ralph's gross estate was $5,250,000. In Ralph's Will, he left his half of the home ($750,000) and condominium ($1,000,000) to his wife, Theresa, and he left everything else he owned to his children. Since his estate received a $1,750,000 deduction for the bequests to his surviving spouse, Ralph's net estate was valued at $3,500,000, and no federal estate tax was due.

Paul A. Rabalais

How to Avoid Capital Gains Tax

When most people think about avoiding taxes at death, they think about how to avoid the federal estate tax. With the estate tax exemption at about $5 million ($10 million for married couples), most families do not have to be concerned about paying federal estate tax.

The tax that often creeps up and bites people is the capital gains tax. Capital gains tax is paid when you sell an asset that has appreciated in value. For example, if you buy stock for $20,000 and later sell the stock for $100,000, you will have $80,000 of capital gain and you must pay tax on this gain.

Step-up in Basis

When you die, the basis of your assets will be "stepped-up." Your heirs will get a new basis. Your heirs' basis will not be what you paid for the asset. Your heirs' basis will be the fair market value of the asset on the date that you died.

Example. Years ago, Jane bought stock in XYZ Company for $50,000. When Jane died many years later, the stock was worth $400,000. Jane left this stock equally to her two children so that each child received stock that was worth $200,000. Since the basis of the stock was stepped-up at death, each child will have a capital gains basis of $200,000 on their share of the stock. If they sell the stock for $200,000 shortly after Jane dies, they will incur no capital gains tax as a result of the sale.

Carry-over Basis

Note that this basis rule is different if you donate appreciated assets during your lifetime. The donee does not receive a step-up in basis on stock that is given to him or her during the donor's lifetime. If, in the previous example, Jane had donated the stock to her two children just prior to Jane's death, the children would each have a basis of $25,000 on their share of the stock, and they would have incurred significant capital gains tax on a subsequent sale of the stock – even if they waited until after Jane died to sell the stock.

For this reason, many people choose to hold on to their appreciated assets and let their heirs inherit them at the stepped-up basis, rather than donating appreciated assets to heirs during life causing donees to have a carry-over basis.

Married Couples and the Capital Gains Tax

How married couples structure their bequests to each other and to their family can have a significant impact on how much capital gains tax heirs will have to pay when appreciated assets are later sold. The fact that there is so much uncertainty about future estate tax laws does not make these decisions any easier.

For starters, be aware of the rule that in community property states like Louisiana, when the first spouse dies all of the community property (yes, I said all of the community property – not just the deceased spouse's share) receives a step-up in basis to the value as of the date of death of the first spouse to die. When the surviving spouse later dies, assets owned by the surviving spouse get stepped-up again.

Example. Richard and Marie have $1 million of community property. Richard died leaving his entire estate to Marie. All of their community property receives a step-up in basis when Richard dies. Marie dies years later when these assets are valued at $2 million. Because Richard left it all to Marie and Marie owned it all at her death, their children will enjoy another step-up in basis on all the family assets. If Richard had left Marie usufruct of his estate, then only Marie's half of the assets would receive another step-up when she died because she did not "own" what was formerly Richard's half.

Bottom line on capital gains tax: Do not forget about potential capital gains tax when planning your estate. It often gets overlooked. Structuring your bequests the wrong way can cost your family hundreds of thousands (or more) of unnecessary capital gains tax.

How Married Couples Avoid Estate Tax

There are many estate tax planning techniques that individuals and married couples can utilize. One of those techniques is to have the Will or trust set up properly to make certain that each married person's estate utilizes its maximum estate tax exemption. This allows married couples who die in 2014 to exempt $10,600,000 from the federal estate tax, because each estate is entitled to a $5,300,000 exemption – but you have to have things set up just right.

The two common ways couples arrange their Wills to avoid estate tax are:

1. Giving your spouse the lifetime usufruct of your estate; or
2. Leaving your estate in a QTIP trust for the benefit of your surviving spouse.

Avoiding Estate Tax by Giving Lifetime Usufruct

Example. Jack and Margaret have community property worth $12,000,000. John died in 2014 with a Will leaving the usufruct of his estate ($6,000,000) to Margaret, and he provided that the usufruct would last for the rest of her lifetime (her usufruct does not terminate upon remarriage). Jack's bequest to Margaret qualifies for special treatment under our Internal Revenue Code. Jack's executor must file a federal estate tax return within nine months after Jack's death. Jack's estate will utilize its approximately $5,000,000 estate tax exemption. The excess $1,000,000 will not be subject to estate tax, but it will be added to Margaret's estate and be subject to estate tax when Margaret dies. No estate tax is due at Jack's death. Margaret now owns her half of the community property (worth $6,000,000) and the amount of Jack's estate in excess of the $5,000,000 estate tax exemption will also be included in Margaret's estate, so Margaret now has a taxable estate of about $7,000,000. When Margaret dies Margaret can use her $5 million estate tax exemption to shield her estate from tax as well.

The lifetime usufruct qualifies for special estate tax treatment. The theory is that married couples who plan properly are not forced to pay federal estate tax when the first spouse dies, regardless of the value of the estate. With proper estate planning and proper estate administration at death, it is fairly simple to avoid estate tax when the first spouse dies. Most estate tax planning for married couples involves avoiding estate tax at the death of the surviving spouse.

Intestate Usufruct – Estate Tax Owed

If in the previous example, Jack had died intestate (without a Will), Margaret would have inherited the usufruct of Jack's community property until her death or remarriage. Since her usufruct would not be for her lifetime only, the usufruct would not qualify for the favorable estate tax treatment and about $500,000 of estate tax would be owed to the IRS within nine months after Jack's death.

Avoiding Estate Tax by Using QTIP Trusts

The second way Louisiana married couples avoid or minimize federal estate tax is to provide that at the first spouse's death, the first spouse's assets remain in trust for the surviving spouse's lifetime. If the trust language provides that the surviving spouse is entitled to the income of the trust assets for the rest of her lifetime, then estate tax can be avoided at the first death, similar to the way tax is avoided when lifetime usufruct is utilized.

QTIP stands for "qualified terminable interest property." Other terms often used in conjunction with this type of trust include credit shelter trust, bypass trust, and marital deduction trust. The terms of these trusts can be spelled out in the deceased's revocable living trust or in the deceased's Last Will and Testament.

Gifts of $14,000

You may have heard that you can donate or give $14,000 (it used to be $10,000) to people each year without tax consequences. Many people are confused by this rule.

Typically no one pays income tax on a gift regardless of the value of the gift. A sizable gift, however, will have gift and estate tax consequences.

Example. Alice gives her daughter, Suzanne, $114,000 on February 1, 2014, to help Suzanne buy a home. This gift has no income tax effect on either Alice or her daughter, Suzanne. No tax is due as a result of the gift. The primary tax effect, however, is that Alice has made a $100,000 taxable gift. Gifts of $14,000 or less each calendar year need not be reported, but the fact that Alice gave $114,000 to Suzanne must be reported on a federal gift tax return (IRS Form 709), showing that Alice has used $100,000 of her $5,300,000 federal estate tax exemption. When Alice dies, her estate tax exemption (the amount exempt from federal estate tax) will be $5,200,000 instead of $5,300,000 because she used part of her estate tax exemption during her lifetime.

Many people who make gifts to others in excess of $14,000 in a calendar year do not have an estate that exceeds the applicable estate tax exemption of $5,300,000, so there really is no tax consequence at all to making large gifts other than the requirement of filing a federal gift tax return disclosing that the gift was made.

Tax Avoidance Techniques

Much has been said and written about avoiding federal estate tax and other taxes at death. The increase in the estate tax exemption to $5,300,000 will exclude many estates from being subject to the tax. However, for those families that are still subject to the estate tax, the following are popular estate tax planning tools:

1. Prepare Your Will or Trust Properly. For many people (especially married couples), having your Last Will and Testament or Revocable Living Trust conform to the estate tax laws will avoid estate tax completely. The lifetime usufruct allows married couples to exempt up to $10,600,000 from estate tax.
2. Annual gifts. You can give away $14,000 to as many people as you want, every year, to reduce your estate. If you have four children and eight grandchildren, you could (if you wanted to) reduce your taxable estate by $168,000 each year by making $14,000 gifts to each of them.
3. Use Life Insurance To Pay Estate Tax. This is a tool made popular by the life insurance industry. You are not reducing your estate tax by purchasing life insurance, but you are making gifts to children or others and the gifted money is used to purchase life insurance on your life that might pay the estate tax liability when you die.

4. Capital Gains Tax. Do not put appreciated assets in your kids' names without first considering the capital gains tax effect. Your heirs will enjoy the step-up in basis only if they inherit assets from you when you die, not if you donate assets to them during your lifetime.
5. Gifts and Bequests To Charity. What you leave to a qualified charity completely avoids estate tax. If Bill Gates and his wife leave their entire estate to their charitable foundation (or any other charity) no estate tax will be due at their deaths. There are many ways to donate or bequeath money to charity – some simple and some complex.

Conclusion

You cannot avoid death, but you may be able to minimize or avoid death tax by:

- Making sure your estate utilizes its $5,300,000 exemption available for deaths occurring in 2014;
- Properly setting up—if you are married—your Will or your Revocable Living Trust so there will be no tax upon the death of the first spouse regardless of the size of the estate;
- Ensuring that your heirs receive a step-up in basis – not just when the first spouse dies but again when the surviving spouse dies;
- Utilizing annual exclusion gifts of $14,000 during your lifetime to reduce your taxable estate at your death.

Chapter 10

Usufruct
What in the Heck Is a Usufruct?

Usufruct is a term used almost exclusively in Louisiana. Very few, if any, of the national books and publications on estate planning even mention the term "usufruct."

However, usufruct is a common term in Louisiana, especially among married couples. When a married person dies, the surviving spouse often inherits the usufruct of the deceased spouse's assets.

Example: Bill and Mary have been married for years. They have two grown children. They have a home worth $200,000, two cars each worth $15,000, 1000 shares of ABC Corp. stock valued at $60,000, and their bank accounts and CDs total $300,000. Bill dies intestate (without a Will). Since Bill died intestate, Mary continues to own her one-half of their community property, and Mary inherits the usufruct of Bill's one-half of the community property until she dies or remarries, whichever occurs first. Bill's children inherit the naked ownership of Bill's half of the community property. What are Mary's rights and obligations as usufructuary, and what are their children's rights and obligations as naked owners?

What Is a Usufruct?

A usufruct is a right that a person has for a certain period of time on the property of another person. The features of the right of usufruct vary with the nature of the things subject to it.

Usufruct of Consumable Things

Consumable things are those that cannot be used without being spent or consumed, such as bank accounts, certificates of deposit (CDs), promissory notes, money market accounts and cash.

If the things subject to the usufruct are consumables, the usufructuary becomes the owner of them. She can spend them or sell them. At the termination of the usufruct, she must give the naked owners the value that the things had at the start of the usufruct.

When Bill died intestate in our example, he and Mary owned $300,000 of bank accounts. Bank accounts are consumable things. Mary continued owning her one-half of these accounts ($150,000), and she inherited the usufruct of Bill's one-half of these accounts ($150,000). Mary can do whatever she wants with the entire $300,000, but at the termination of the usufruct—when she dies or remarries—she (or her estate) must pay to the naked owners (Bill's children) a total of $150,000. Even if Mary invested the $300,000 and caused it to increase to $500,000, she still owes the children a total of $150,000 at the termination of the usufruct. If Mary spent some of the $300,000 so that at the termination of the usufruct there was only $175,000 left, she still owes Bill's children a total of $150,000.

Usufruct of Non-Consumable Things

Non-consumable things are those that may be enjoyed without alteration of their substance, although their substance may be diminished or deteriorated naturally by time or by the use to which they are applied. Common examples of non-consumable things include:

- Land
- Houses
- Shares of stock
- Animals
- Furniture
- Vehicles

If the things subject to usufruct are non-consumables, the usufructuary has the right to possess them and to derive the utility, profits, and advantages that they may produce, under the obligation of preserving their substance. The usufructuary is bound to use the non-consumable things as a prudent administrator and to deliver them to the naked owner at the termination of the usufruct.

In our example on the first page of this chapter, the home, stock, and vehicles are non-consumable things. Let's look at each one individually:

Usufruct of Home

After Bill dies, Mary owns an undivided one-half interest in the home, she has the usufruct of half the home, and Bill's two children are naked owners of half the home. While Mary is living there after Bill's death, the property increases in value from $200,000 to $300,000. When Mary dies, Bill's children own half the home, and half the home is in Mary's estate (she may also leave her half of the home to the two children).

Usufruct of Stock

After Bill died, Mary owned 500 shares of stock herself, and she had the usufruct of 500 shares of stock. Bill's children were naked owners of 500 shares. If Mary never sells the usufruct shares, the children will own the 500 shares at the termination of the usufruct. The naked owners will benefit if the stock appreciates in value, but they will lose out if the stock depreciates in value.

Usufruct Stock Is Sold

When Bill died, Mary had the usufruct of 500 shares of stock, and those shares were worth $30,000. Five years later those shares are worth $80,000 and Mary sells those 500 shares over which she has the usufruct for $80,000. Mary just converted a non-consumable thing (stock) into a consumable thing (cash). She now has a usufruct of the cash ($80,000). She can do whatever she wants with the cash but at the termination of the usufruct (her death or remarriage) she owes the naked owners (Bill's children) $80,000, less any tax paid as a result of the sale.

Usufruct of Vehicles

In our example, Bill and Mary owned two vehicles each worth $15,000. Since these vehicles were community property, Mary owns half of each of these vehicles, she has the usufruct of half of each vehicle, and Bill's children are naked owners of half of each vehicle.

Mary sells one vehicle after Bill dies for $8,000, and she keeps the other vehicle for the rest of her lifetime. When she dies, her estate owes Bill's children a total of $4,000 (half of the proceeds from the sale of one vehicle), and Bill's children will own half of the vehicle that Mary owned when she died. If those two children were Mary's sole heirs, they will own the entire vehicle, because they will inherit Mary's half.

Donation of Thing Subject to Usufruct

If the right to donate property was expressly granted to the usufructuary, the usufructuary may donate a non-consumable item subject to usufruct. If a thing subject to usufruct is donated by the usufructuary, the usufructuary is obligated to pay the value the thing had at the time it was donated to the naked owner at the termination of the usufruct.

Example: Dad owned a home. Dad died leaving Wife the usufruct of his home for her lifetime, and Dad expressly stated in his Will that Wife could donate the home. Dad named his only child (Eric) as the naked owner. Shortly after Dad dies, Wife donates the home to her only child (Holly). At the time of the donation, the home is worth $250,000. When Wife dies, her estate owes Eric $250,000, which was the value of the home at the time it was donated to Holly.

Establishing Usufruct

Usufructs are often established when someone dies. For example, a married person may, in his Will, leave his surviving spouse the usufruct of everything he owns when he dies. Or, if a married person dies without a will, the deceased's surviving spouse will inherit the usufruct of all the deceased's half of the community property.

Myth: When a married person dies intestate, one half of their half of the community property goes to the children and one-half of their half goes to the spouse.

Truth: When a married person dies intestate, all of the deceased's half of the community property goes in naked ownership to the deceased's children, subject to the usufruct of the surviving spouse until the earlier to occur of death or remarriage.

A usufruct may also be established during one's lifetime. For example, parents may donate their home to their children during the parents' lifetime by signing an Act of Donation, but the document may reflect that the parents are retaining the lifetime usufruct of the home.

Usufruct to Successive Usufructuaries

Some parents want a child or other loved one to be able to live in the home after the parents die, but when the child has no more use for the home, they want the home to be co-owned by all of their children. So, a parent may leave his spouse the usufruct of his half of the home in his Will and also provide that a child will have a successive usufruct of the home after the surviving spouse dies. This is permitted under Louisiana law.

Usufructuary Rights

The usufructuary is entitled to the "use" and "fruits" of the thing subject to the usufruct. The following are some examples explaining the rights of the usufructuary:

- A cash dividend on stock subject to usufruct belongs to the usufructuary;
- The usufructuary has the right to vote shares of stock;
- The usufructuary may make improvements and alterations on property with written consent of the naked owner;
- When the usufruct includes timberlands, the usufructuary is bound to manage them prudently. Proceeds from properly managed timber operations belong to the usufructuary;
- Since the usufructuary is the owner of cash, they are also the owner of any interest that the cash, CDs, or savings account produces.

Usufructuary Obligations

The usufructuary may have numerous obligations, such as the obligation to provide security, the responsibility to provide repairs, the payment of necessary expenses, taxes, debts, and other charges.

Obligation of Usufructuary to Provide Security

Example: James and Florence are married. James had two children from a prior marriage. James and Florence have community property. James dies intestate (without a Will). Florence inherits the usufruct of James' one-half of the community property, and James' two children are the naked owners of James' half of the community property. Since the usufructuary (Florence) is not the parent of James' two children, those children can force Florence to provide security. This security will protect James' two children in the event Florence spends, neglects, or wanders off with the property over which she has usufruct.

Usufructuary's Standard of Care

The usufructuary is answerable for losses resulting from his fraud, default, or neglect. The following are common usufructuary obligations:

- The usufructuary is responsible for ordinary maintenance and repairs;
- The naked owner is responsible for extraordinary repairs unless resulting from usufructuary fault or neglect. Extraordinary repairs are those for the reconstruction of the whole or a substantial part of the property subject to usufruct. All other repairs are ordinary.

Property Totally Destroyed

If a hurricane or other act totally destroys property that is subject to usufruct, neither the usufructuary nor the naked owner is bound to restore property totally destroyed through accident or because of age.

Usufructuary Responsibility for Charges and Debts

The usufructuary is bound to pay property taxes on the property subject to usufruct.

The usufructuary may remove all improvements he has made, subject to the obligation of restoring the property to its former condition. The usufructuary may not claim compensation from the naked owner for improvements that the usufructuary does not remove or that cannot be removed.

Naked Owner Rights and Obligations

In our previous example, James' two children are naked owners of their father's estate, and Florence has the usufruct of those assets. James' children have a number of rights and obligations.

The naked owners may sell their naked ownership interest. Perhaps Florence wants to own the home that she and James owned together. She could purchase her former step-children's naked ownership interest.

Usually a naked ownership interest is not very marketable, because the new naked owner's interest will continue to be burdened by the usufruct. The naked owner must not interfere with the rights of the usufructuary, and the naked owner may not make changes or improvements on the property subject to the usufruct.

Usufruct Termination

A person's usufruct terminates upon their death, unless it is established for a term or subject to a condition and that term expires or that condition happens.

Example: Roy owned his home prior to marrying Alice. Roy's home was his separate property. Roy's Will left his home to his three children, subject to Alice having the usufruct of his home until she either died or remarried. In 2000, Alice continued living in the home as usufructuary after Roy died. On June 1, 2004, Alice married again. As of June 1, 2004, Roy's three children owned "full ownership" of the home. Alice would have no more right to occupy the home.

Insurance Proceeds

When proceeds of insurance are due on account of loss, extinction, or destruction of property subject to usufruct, the usufruct attaches to the insurance proceeds.

Example: A hurricane destroys property over which Alice has a usufruct and Bob, Carol, and David are naked owners. The insurance company pays Alice $120,000 for the property damage. When the usufruct terminates, Alice owes Bob, Carol, and David $40,000 each.

Usufructuary Abuses Enjoyment

Example: After Roy dies, Alice has the usufruct of his home, and Bob, Carol, and David are naked owners. Alice neglects the home to the extent that it becomes used as a hangout for drug dealers. What rights do Bob, Carol, and David have? They may get a court to rule that the Alice's usufruct is terminated because Alice committed waste, she neglected to make ordinary repairs, or she abused her enjoyment in any other manner.

Settling up with the Naked Owners

Example. After Roy died, Alice had the lifetime usufruct of $600,000 in bank accounts. Roy's three children (who were not Alice's children) were the naked owners. The three naked owners knew they would not get any money until Alice died. Alice did not like the fact that she felt like Roy's three children were hoping she would die so they could get their inheritance. Alice decided she had enough other money to live off of for the rest of her life, so she renounced her usufruct and allowed Roy's children to receive their inheritance.

Other Rights Similar to Usufruct

There are two other rights that are similar to usufruct in Louisiana: the right of habitation and the right of use.

Right of Habitation

The right of habitation is the right of a person to live in the house of another. Only individuals may have a right of habitation, and the right of habitation may be established in houses only. The right of habitation is more narrow than the usufruct.

Right of Use

The right of use gives a person or entity the right to use certain things. Common examples of rights of use include:

- A right of passage over property,
- A right of light and view,
- The right to fish or hunt,
- The right to take fruits or products from property.

Conclusion

Remember the following regarding the Louisiana usufruct:

- The usufruct is common in Louisiana but uncommon or non-existent in all other states;
- When you leave your spouse the usufruct of assets, you also designate who the "naked owners" are who will get the assets at the termination of the usufruct;
- The usufructuary's rights vary depending on whether the usufructuary has the usufruct of a consumable item (such as cash) or a non-consumable item (such as real estate or shares of stock).

Chapter 11

Living Wills
Making Your Wishes Known about Life Support Machines

You have the right to control decisions relating to your own medical care, including the decision to have life-sustaining procedures withheld or withdrawn in instances where you are diagnosed as having a terminal and irreversible condition.

The Louisiana legislature has determined that the artificial prolongation of life for a person diagnosed as having a terminal and irreversible condition may cause loss of individual and personal dignity which secures a burdensome existence while providing nothing medically necessary or beneficial to the person.

It is difficult to make a decision to authorize the withdrawal of life support machines for someone you love. The purpose of our living will laws is to allow you to tell your family and your doctors what your wishes are regarding life support machines so your family does not have to make that final decision. You have made your decision for them in advance by signing your living will.

Estate Planning in Louisiana

Making a Living Will

You may make, at any time, a written living will (also known as a "declaration") that directs the withholding or withdrawal of life-sustaining procedures if you have a terminal and irreversible condition.

Your written living will must be signed by you in the presence of two witnesses. The witnesses must not be related to you by blood or marriage, and a witness must not be someone who would inherit from you when you die.

Oral Living Will

An adult may make an oral or non-verbal living will in the presence of two witnesses by any non-written means of communication at any time after the diagnosis of a terminal and irreversible condition.

Sample Living Will

The Louisiana Legislature has created a sample form for a living will. Your living will may include other specific directions including but not limited to a designation of someone else to make your treatment decisions if you are not capable of communicating your wishes.

DECLARATION

Declaration made this _____ day of _____ 20__.

I, _____, being of sound mind, willfully and voluntarily make known my desire that my dying shall not be artificially prolonged under the circumstances set forth below and do hereby declare:

If at any time I should have an incurable injury, disease, or illness, or be in a continual profound comatose state with no reasonable chance of recovery, certified to be a terminal and irreversible condition by two physicians who have personally examined me, one of whom shall be my attending physician, and the physicians have determined that my death will occur whether or not life-sustaining procedures are utilized and where the application of life-sustaining procedures would serve only to prolong artificially the dying process, I direct (initial only one)

_____ that all life-sustaining procedures, including nutrition and hydration, be withheld or withdrawn so that food and water will not be administered invasively,

_____ that life-sustaining procedures, except nutrition and hydration, be withheld or withdrawn so that food and water can be administered invasively,

and that I be permitted to die naturally with only the administration of medication or the performance of any medical procedure deemed necessary to provide me with comfort care.

I further direct that I be permitted to die naturally with only the administration of medication or the performance of any medical procedure deemed necessary to provide me with comfort care.

In the absence of my ability to give directions regarding the use of such life-sustaining procedures, it is my intention that this declaration shall be honored by my family and physician(s) as the final expression of my legal right to refuse medical or surgical treatment, and I accept the consequences of such refusal.

I understand the full import of this declaration, and I am emotionally and mentally competent to make this declaration.

_____

Your Name

City___, Louisiana

The declarant has been personally known to me, and I believe him or her to be of sound mind.

_____

WITNESS

_____

WITNESS

Life-Sustaining Procedure

What is a "life-sustaining procedure?" It is defined as any medical procedure or intervention which, within reasonable medical judgment, would serve only to prolong the dying process for a person diagnosed as having a terminal and irreversible condition. The term includes such procedures as the invasive administration of nutrition. A "life-sustaining procedure" does not include any measure deemed necessary to provide comfort care.

Revoking Your Living Will

You may revoke your living will at any time by doing any of the following:

- Destroying your living will or by directing some other person to destroy your living will,
- Writing a revocation expressing your intent to revoke your living will. You must sign and date the revocation,
- By making an oral or nonverbal expression of your intent to revoke your living will. This type of revocation becomes effective upon communication to your attending physician.

If No Living Will Exists

It is common for people who have never signed a living will to enter a terminal and irreversible condition. When this occurs, the following individuals have priority to make your life-support decision, in the following order:

1. Any person previously designated by the patient by written instrument in the presence of two witnesses to have the authority to make the living will if the patient is unable
2. The court appointed legal guardian of the patient if one has been appointed
3. The patient's spouse
4. An adult child of the patient

5. The parents of the patient
6. The patient's sibling
7. The patient's other ascendants or descendants.

Do Not Resuscitate Identification Bracelet

If you register your living will with the secretary of state and pay a fee of $20.00, you will be issued a "do not resuscitate" bracelet which will include your name, date of birth, and the phrase "DO NOT RESUSCITATE."

Certified emergency medical technicians or certified first responders can be held criminally or civilly liable if they withhold life-sustaining procedures. However, if they discover that you are wearing a Do Not Resuscitate Identification Bracelet, they cannot be subject to liability for withholding life-sustaining procedures.

Chapter 12

Trusts
Trusts Can Be Great Tools - When Used for the Right Reasons

Trusts are complicated to the lay person. When used properly, they can be a valuable estate planning tool. Some of the common uses for trusts include: avoiding probate, minimizing federal estate tax, protecting your children from squandering their inheritance, providing for grandchildren's education or other needs, protecting your spouse from your children of a previous marriage, protecting your children of a previous marriage from your spouse, protecting the inheritance of a special needs child, and much more.

What Is a Trust?

A trust is defined as a relationship that results when someone transfers title to an asset to a person whose job it is to administer it for another.

Example: In George's Will, he made a bequest of $50,000 to his son, George, Jr., as trustee of a trust for the benefit of George's grandson, George III. George provided, among other things, that the principal of the trust could be used for the health and education of George III. George also provided that if the assets had not been used by the time George III reached the age of thirty the trust would terminate, and the remaining trust assets would be distributed to George III. When George later died, a trust account was established, and George, Jr., managed the account as trustee.

Who Are the People Involved in a trust?

Every trust has one or more settlors, trustees, and beneficiaries. The Settlor is typically the person who sets up the trust. In the previous example, George is the Settlor. The Trustee is the person who manages the trust assets. In our previous example, George, Jr., is the Trustee. The beneficiary is the person who benefits from the trust. George III is the beneficiary in our previous example.

What Are the Most Common Uses of Trusts?

There are many uses for trusts in Louisiana. The following are some of the more popular uses of trusts.

Revocable Living Trust

While the revocable living trust has been a popular estate planning tool around the United States for decades, its popularity in Louisiana has intensified in recent years. Generally there are three reasons why the revocable living trust is a popular estate planning tool.

1. The properly funded living trust avoids attorney costs and court costs involved in settling your estate through the court-supervised Louisiana succession;
2. Distributing assets after death to beneficiaries of a living trust is faster than distributing assets to heirs in a Louisiana succession; and
3. A Louisiana succession requires a detailed public listing of all of your assets and debts when you die. A living trust can be settled without the necessity of a public detailed listing of your assets and debts.

What Is a Revocable Living Trust?

Example: Charlene has three children. Charlene went through a difficult and lengthy succession when her father died and she wants to make sure that her children do not have to go through a similar process when she dies. Charlene sets up a revocable living trust, naming her three children as equal beneficiaries at her death. Charlene names herself as the initial trustee, and she names her daughter, Karen, as the successor trustee to be in charge when Charlene dies. Charlene reserves the right to change or revoke her trust at any time. Charlene transfers her real estate and her investments to her trust. When Charlene dies, Karen immediately disburses the investments and the real estate equally to Charlene's three children. No succession was necessary, because no assets were titled in Charlene's name that would require succession court orders to transfer.

The revocable living trust is used primarily as a succession avoidance tool. Assets that are titled in your name when you die will be frozen, and your family will have to go through a succession to obtain court orders that will order banks, financial institutions, and others to transfer your assets to your heirs. If your assets are titled in the name of your trust, your successor trustee will have immediate access to your assets and will be able to sell or distribute them to the beneficiaries you named in your trust. No succession will be necessary to transfer these assets after your death.

Avoiding the Louisiana Succession

Many years ago it was determined that the courts must oversee the distribution of a deceased person's assets to their heirs. In Louisiana, this court-supervised procedure is known as a "succession." All other states call this process "probate."

Having the courts oversee the distribution of your estate to your heirs may not be the most efficient way for your family to settle your estate. Courts are well known for having inherent delays and costs.

In most living trust arrangements, the parents are the Settlors, the initial Trustees, and the first income beneficiaries. A successor trustee or co-trustees are designated (often an adult child or children), and the children are designated as the principal beneficiaries to receive the trust assets after the parents die. When the parents die, trust assets are not frozen, and trust assets do not have to go through a court-supervised succession procedure to be transferred. The trust instrument and trust law permit the successor trustee to distribute the trust assets in accordance with the instructions provided in the trust instrument.

What Savings Result from Avoiding a Succession?

That is a difficult question to answer. There is no standard for succession costs in Louisiana. Succession costs always include court filing costs and attorney fees. There is no standard for attorney fees.

You can ask five different attorneys how they charge for a succession and you may get five completely different answers. Where families get taken advantage of is when there is not a crystal clear discussion regarding attorney fees at the outset.

I met with a woman once who, after her husband died, went to see an attorney who went to her church. She asked him to handle her husband's succession. They did not discuss fees. When he finished months later, he sent her a bill for $35,000. She said she does not speak to this attorney any more even though they go to the same church.

Tip: Always work with an attorney who provides you with a fixed fee quote – in writing – prior to commencing the legal services.

Bottom line: Let's assume that completing the Louisiana successions – first after the husband dies, and again after the wife dies - costs $15,000 after each death. This means that if the succession is avoided by using a revocable living trust, the family will save around $30,000.

More Savings If You Own Out-of-State Real Estate

If you live in Louisiana and you own real estate in another state when you die, your heirs will have to go through a succession in Louisiana, and they will also have to go through an "ancillary probate" in the other state. The Louisiana succession transfers your Louisiana real estate and all other non-real estate assets. The Louisiana succession does not transfer out-of-state real estate. A probate in that other state must occur to transfer that property to your heirs.

If you have a revocable living trust and you transfer your out-of-state real estate to your trust, this ancillary probate will be avoided.

Living Trust Settlement Faster than Succession

Example: Dad died owning two investment accounts. Each account held about $300,000 of investments. One account was titled in Dad's name. The other account was titled in the name of Dad's revocable living trust. After Dad died, the successor trustee of Dad's trust was given immediate access to the trust account and within one week was able to distribute the account to Dad's beneficiaries. The account that was titled in Dad's name, however, had to go through a succession with the family incurring thousands in costs. It took several months for the succession paperwork to make its way through the judge's office, the processing department at the courthouse, and the legal department of the institution which held Dad's account.

Let's look at a typical example of the mechanics of a revocable living trust and how it should work in Louisiana. Let's say you are married and you have three children. You feel it would be in you and your family's best interests to form a revocable living trust. Here is what happens next.

You work with an attorney (hopefully an attorney knowledgeable in living trusts and hopefully someone with whom you have good rapport) to prepare your revocable living trust. A complete revocable living trust estate plan will also include a Last Will and Testament for you and your spouse, a durable property power of attorney, a health care power of attorney, a living will declaration, and legal documents transferring your Louisiana real estate to your trust. Once all these documents are prepared, you sign them.

Next, you must fund the trust. You will avoid probate only if all of your "probate assets" have been transferred to your trust before your death. Documents are prepared and signed whereby you and your spouse transfer title to your home, other real estate, stock, bonds, brokerage accounts, and mineral interests to your trust. The real estate transfers must be recorded in the public records of the parish where the property is located. Louisiana law also provides that if the trust owns real estate, the entire trust or a summary extract must be recorded in the public records of the parish where the property is located.

Which Assets Do Not Need to Be Transferred to Your Revocable Living Trust?

It is likely that you own assets that do not need to be transferred to your trust, and probate can still be avoided.

IRAs, 401(k) accounts, annuities, and life insurance policies have designated beneficiaries. By their nature, these types of accounts avoid probate. As long as you properly designate beneficiaries, these assets will not be part of your "probate estate" when you die, and your beneficiaries will not be required to go through a succession when you die to obtain ownership of these funds.

Example. Dad owns an IRA. He names Mom as the primary beneficiary, and he names his two children as equal contingent beneficiaries. When Dad dies, Mom obtains a death certificate and presents it to the financial institution where Dad's IRA is held. Dad's IRA will be transferred into Mom's IRA without a court proceeding.

Do Vehicles Need to Be Transferred to My Revocable Living Trust?

There is an easier way. Dad may have a revocable living trust so his wife and children avoid probate. However, as long as Dad has his Last Will set up correctly, Dad can keep his vehicles in his name and his family will avoid probate.

The Louisiana Office of Motor Vehicles will transfer title of a vehicle after death if a **copy** of a Will is produced after the death of the owner.

Example. Dad owns three vehicles. Dad has a living trust that owns his real estate and his non-IRA investments. Dad leaves his vehicles in his own name but when Dad has his trust prepared he also has a Will prepared that leaves his vehicles to Mom. After Dad dies, Mom produces a copy of Dad's Will to the Office of Motor Vehicles, and they re-title the vehicles into Mom's name without needing any succession court orders.

Do You Need to Transfer Your Bank Accounts to Your Revocable Living Trust?

There are two schools of thought on whether you should transfer your bank accounts to your revocable living trust if your goal is to avoid the Louisiana succession.

You can go to your bank and set up new trust bank accounts. You will close your accounts that are in your name and operate out of the new trust accounts. This may be cumbersome, particularly if you have several automatic deposits and withdrawals that must be changed to the new account.

Or, if you want to make it simpler, you can leave your bank accounts in your name and take your successor trustee (or some other trusted person) to your bank and give them signature authority on your bank accounts. Now, when you die (or when you and your spouse die), the person to whom you gave signature authority will have the ability to access your accounts to pay for your funeral, pay other expenses, and divide the money among the beneficiaries of your revocable living trust.

What Happens to a Revocable Living Trust When the First Spouse Dies?

How your trust works after the first spouse dies (if you are married and you and your spouse set up a trust) depends on how you set up the trust in the first place.

You could have set up your trust so the entire trust is now controlled by the surviving spouse, and the surviving spouse can revoke or change any provisions of the entire trust.

Or, you could have set up your trust so that when one spouse dies, that spouse's share of the trust becomes irrevocable. This protects the beneficiaries of the first spouse to die.

Example. Dad dies after Dad and Mom created a revocable living trust. Dad has three of his own children from his first marriage. Mom has two children from a prior marriage. When Dad dies, their joint trust assets total $1 million in value. Dad's part of the trust ($500,000) becomes irrevocable. Mom can do whatever she wants with her half, and she continues to be the trustee of Dad's half. She can spend Dad's half if she needs it, but whatever is left in Dad's half when Mom later dies must go to Dad's three children. Also, the assets in the "Dad Trust" will not be included in Mom's estate for federal estate tax purposes.

When the surviving spouse dies, the successor trustee (likely your adult child) will be responsible for following the instructions you gave them in the trust for terminating the trust and distributing trust assets to the beneficiaries. If the surviving spouse, at the time of his or her death, owns shares of stock, real estate, or other "probate assets" in his or name (as opposed to being owned by the trust) a succession will be necessary to transfer the assets out of the decedent's name to the trust pursuant to the "pour-over Will." If the trust was funded properly the "pour-over Will" may never need to be used.

The following are important points about revocable living trusts in Louisiana:

- Taxes. Typically you and your family will pay no more or less taxes if you have a revocable living trust. All trust income flows through the trust to you personally. The trust pays no tax;
- Funding. It is important that you transfer assets to your trust during your lifetime. Typical assets you must transfer to your trust include your real estate (both in Louisiana and out of state, mineral interests, stocks, bonds, and mutual funds);
- Assets You Can Keep in Your Name. Keep your IRAs, 401(k)s, annuities, and life insurance in your name, but designate beneficiaries on a designated beneficiary form;
- Save Time and Estate Settlement Costs. The succession/probate procedure in the state of Louisiana takes months if not years. Using a revocable living trust to avoid a Louisiana

succession can save your loved ones the cost, stress, and inherent delays involved in a succession;

- Work With an Expert. Louisiana has its own trust code that is different from all other state trust codes. The trust laws change annually. Make sure you work with a Louisiana attorney who is familiar with the nuances of the Louisiana Trust Code and succession law.

The following people are typically eager to establish a revocable living trust in Louisiana:

- You have been through a difficult Louisiana succession or an out-of-state probate in the past – perhaps when your parents died – and you do not want to put your loved ones through the same thing;
- Perhaps your parents had a revocable living trust when they died, and you saw how easy it was to settle their estate;
- You do not want your spouse or children to go through an expensive, time-consuming, stressful, and public court process when you die;
- You live in Louisiana but you own real estate in other states. A revocable living trust will avoid the Louisiana succession and the ancillary probate in those other states where you own real estate;
- You want someone else to manage your assets for you. You can establish your revocable living trust and name someone else as your trustee (such as a trusted friend, advisor, relative, or a

corporate trustee) so they can handle your investments, bank accounts, and also handle purchases and sales of assets on your behalf.

While the determination of whether you should have a Will-based estate plan or a trust-based estate plan depends on your circumstances and objectives, it is fair to state that your Will-based plan is easy to set up but requires court supervision of your estate settlement. Alternatively, a trust-based plan requires you to transfer assets to your trust during your lifetime but avoids court interference when you die.

Other Uses for Trusts

Trusts for Minors

If you have minor children, or if you plan on leaving a bequest to your young grandchildren, you should consider a trust.

In Louisiana, if a minor (a child under the age of 18) inherits in his or her own name, then a court-supervised tutorship proceeding is necessary. The court will appoint a tutor to oversee the minor's inheritance, and the court must approve any payments to or on behalf of the minor in advance. This is an expensive and cumbersome proceeding.

If you have minor children, you might form a trust that states that any inheritance your children receive will be held in trust so the trustee you name can manage the assets and use them for the right reasons without having to get the courts involved.

If you would like to leave bequests to your grandchildren, you should do the same, particularly if your grandchildren are young and unable to manage an inheritance for themselves.

Example. Grandma and Grandpa want to leave $50,000 to each of their five grandchildren (who currently range in age from 15 down to two). If the grandchildren inherit this money while they are minors, a tutorship proceeding will be required in which the court will appoint a tutor to oversee the funds. If the money needs to be used prior to the grandchild's 18th birthday, a judge must approve the expenditure. At the grandchild's 18th birthday, the tutor must turn the funds over to the grandchild.

A better alternative is to provide in Grandma and Grandpa's estate planning documents that these funds for the grandchildren will be placed in trust after the death of Grandma and Grandpa. Perhaps each grandchild's parents could be the trustees of the trust, and Grandma and Grandpa would authorize the trustees to use the funds for the grandchild's health, education and welfare. Perhaps Grandma and Grandpa could also provide that whatever funds remained in the trust when the grandchild reached the age of 25 (or some other age when it is more likely that the grandchild would have matured) would be turned over to the grandchild.

Trusts to Avoid Estate Taxes

The federal estate tax exemption has increased in recent years from $600,000 to $5,340,000. Less than 1% of families are subject to the federal estate tax.

Paul A. Rabalais

However, for those families that are subject to this tax, it can be devastating.

Many individuals and couples who are facing a federal estate tax at their deaths transfer assets to an irrevocable trust during their lifetime to remove those assets from their estate. Each person can transfer $14,000 each year either to an individual or to a trust for the benefit of that individual.

Example. Mom and Dad have a combined estate of $13,000,000. Even with a properly drafted Will or revocable living trust, there will be an estate tax bill due to the IRS of about $1,000,000 after the death of the surviving spouse. They have three children and seven grandchildren. Since both Mom and Dad can transfer $14,000 to an unlimited number of people each year tax free, they decide to create an irrevocable trust for the benefit of their children and grandchildren, and they transfer assets valued at $260,000 each year to the trust. They name their wise, responsible son as the trustee of the trust. It will be his job to manage the trust assets until Mom and Dad die, and then distribute the trust assets in accordance with the instructions given by the trust instrument.

Special Needs Trusts

Individuals with certain disabilities can receive cash benefits and medical coverage from various government programs. In order to qualify for these benefits, the individual's income and resources must not exceed certain levels.

If a parent leaves a bequest to a special needs child, the inherited assets may preclude the child from receiving the benefits. The government, however, has established rules to allow assets to be held in trust for the benefit of a special needs child, preserving the government benefits, as long as certain parameters are met.

These trusts, called special needs trusts, preserve government benefit eligibility and leave assets that will meet certain needs of a special needs individual.

Special needs trusts are typically designed so the trust assets can be used to supplement, not supplant, government benefits. Trust assets are typically distributed to third parties to pay for items other than the food and shelter of the disabled individual.

Trusts for Married Couples

Married couples commonly use trusts. Many married couples would like for the surviving spouse to benefit from the assets accumulated during the lifetime of the couple, but married people do not like the idea of all of their assets going to the surviving spouse's "new" spouse.

Example. Ted and Angela have $1,000,000 in assets. These assets are community property because they were accumulated during their marriage. Ted has two children from a prior marriage. Angela has one child from her prior marriage. Ted wants Angela to have access to their estate if he dies first, but he fears it will all be left to Angela's "new" husband if Angela remarries after Ted's death. Or, if Angela does not remarry, she might leave the entire estate to her one child when she dies—to the exclusion of Ted's children. So, Ted establishes a trust (this trust can be in his Will or it can be a stand-alone trust) so Ted's half of the community property goes to the trust when Ted dies. Angela will be able to use the trust property after Ted dies for her health, education, maintenance, and support, but when Angela dies, the remaining trust assets will revert back to Ted's children.

This arrangement of providing for the needs of your spouse while also providing for a future bequest to your children can also be accomplished without a trust by leaving the usufruct of assets to your spouse and naming your children as the naked owners. You do not read about the "usufruct and naked ownership" planning tool in national publications, because Louisiana is the only state that has this form of ownership. However, in Louisiana, leaving your spouse the usufruct of your assets may be the most common form of a bequest between married couples.

Charitable Trusts

You can donate assets to charity during your lifetime. You can also leave assets to a charity when you die by naming them in your trust or on your beneficiary designation forms.

If you donate assets to a charity while you are alive, you may benefit from a charitable income tax deduction, but you will receive no further financial benefit.

If you leave assets to a charity when you die, your estate is entitled to a charitable estate tax deduction, but you get no tax or other financial benefits while you are alive.

If you create a charitable remainder trust during your lifetime and transfer assets to it, you will receive a charitable income tax deduction when you transfer assets to the trust, and the trust, within certain parameters, will pay you an income for the rest of your lifetime or for a certain period of years. Since the trust is a "charitable" trust, it can sell the assets that you transferred to it without incurring any capital gains tax on the appreciation. At your death or at the end of a term, the assets are transferred to your favorite charity or charities.

Conclusion

While trusts can be confusing at first to the lay person, they can be a valuable estate planning tool. Common types of trusts in Louisiana include:

- Revocable Living Trusts. Becoming increasingly popular for Louisiana residents because they allow families to avoid the court-supervised succession procedure at death and provide for a faster and less-costly estate settlement at death. A revocable living trust can be extra beneficial if you own real estate in other states allowing your family to avoid multiple probates.
- Trusts for Minors. If there is a chance your minor child or grandchild will inherit assets from you, then you need to make sure those

assets will be placed in trust so the courts will not need to supervise the minor's assets and so that the minor will be protected from squandering the assets when he or she reaches the age of 18.

- Trusts to Avoid Estate Tax. Not as popular now since the estate tax exemption has increased from $600,000 to $5,340,000, but if estate taxes are likely, you need to consider these irrevocable trusts.

- Special Needs Trust. If you have a child with special needs, make sure any inheritance you leave that child is placed in a special needs trust. This will help preserve government benefits for the child.

- Trusts for Married Couples. A way to make your assets available for your spouse after you die, but when your spouse later dies, the trust assets will revert back to *your* heirs, not your spouse's heirs.

- Charitable Trust. A vehicle that allows you to transfer appreciated assets to a charity, have them sold with no tax consequences, receive an income off those assets for your lifetime, and at your death the remaining trust assets are passed along to your favorite charity or charities.

Chapter 13

Medicaid Planning
Avoid Nursing Home Poverty

What Is Medicaid?

Most of the nursing home residents in Louisiana have their stay paid for, all or in part, by Medicaid. The cost of a monthly nursing home stay in Louisiana can vary from city to city but most nursing homes cost about $6,000 each month. If a married couple is in a nursing home, and they are paying for their care and their medicines and other necessary living expenses, they could be paying out more than $12,000 each month.

An extended nursing home stay can wipe out a family's entire life savings in a few months or a few short years. This is why so many people are interested in finding out how they can qualify for Medicaid, which pays this nursing home cost.

In order to qualify for Medicaid, you must meet Medicaid's definition of "poor." There are other requirements as well – you must be at least 65 years old, blind or disabled, and your income and assets must be limited.

Estate Planning in Louisiana

Title XIX of the Social Security Act, enacted by the Social Security Amendments of 1965, provided for grants to states to implement the Medicaid Program. Medicaid is a federal-state entitlement program that pays for medical services on behalf of low-income eligible persons. Medicaid is financed from federal and state funds.

The Louisiana Department of Health and Hospitals (DHH) is the single state agency under the Louisiana State Plan for administration of medical benefits. The Louisiana Department of Health and Hospitals has a Medical Care Advisory Committee (MCAC), which is mandated by Title XIX regulations. The MCAC consists of 25 people and includes state legislators, physicians and other representatives of the health professions, members of consumer groups, including the Title XIX recipients and consumer organizations, and the Secretary of the Department of Health and Hospitals or his designee.

The vast majority of Medicaid spending for long-term care is on nursing homes. However, Medicaid is available to people who need the type of medical care available in a nursing home setting but who can be treated effectively at home or in the community without being placed in a nursing home. However, Medicaid's resources are limited, and there are long waiting lists to receive these Home and Community Based Waiver services.

Paul A. Rabalais

Medicaid Is Not Medicare!

Even though the names sound similar, the programs are very different. Medicare is the health insurance that most people age 65 and older have in the United States. Medicare is designed to cover the expenses that health insurance typically covers, such as doctor's visits, hospital stays, surgery, and lab tests.

How Does an Unmarried Person Become Eligible for Medicaid?

To be eligible for Medicaid, you must pass an income test and an asset test. Let's look first at the income test.

In Louisiana, a Medicaid applicant can currently have no more than $2,163 of income per month and qualify for Medicaid. But what if your income is $2,300 and the cost of care is $5,000 per month? In Louisiana, you generally qualify for Medicaid from an income point of view if your income is less than your cost of care.

Personal Needs Allowance. The amount of money from your income that you are allowed to keep each month is called the personal needs allowance. Louisiana's personal needs allowance is currently $38. All of your other income, with a few exceptions such as health insurance premiums, must be paid to the nursing home. The nursing home then bills Louisiana's Medicaid program for the shortfall.

Asset Test. A single applicant can have no more than $2,000 of "countable" assets. Countable assets include cash, bank accounts, certificates of deposit, IRAs, 401(k) accounts, stocks, bonds, lump sum annuities, cash value in life insurance policies, real estate that is not your home, business interests, and other assets that can be converted to cash. Interests in a succession are countable even if the succession has not been opened or the inheritance is refused. Usufructs are also countable.

What Assets Do Not Count for Medicaid?

Countable assets, like the ones described above, are assets that count in terms of qualifying for Medicaid. Non-countable assets, also known as excludable assets, do not count. Owning non-countable assets will not affect your Medicaid eligibility.

By far the biggest non-countable asset that most of us own is our home property. In Louisiana, the home property is property in which you have an ownership interest and that serves as your primary residence. It includes the house or lot which is your usual residence, all contiguous property, and any other buildings on the home property. Property is contiguous to the residence if it is touching the residential property (even corner to corner) and is not separated by property owned by others. Property separated by a public right-of-way, such as a road, is considered contiguous.

Do not rely on Homestead Exemption status for determining home property for Medicaid eligibility purposes.

Your home property will be excluded if you are living in your home, or if you are away from your home because of a medical condition, and you are keeping your home available, and you intend to use it as your home when your condition permits. Your home property is also excluded when you are away from your home and your spouse and/or dependant relative lives there.

Your home property is no longer excludable if offered for sale based on your lack of intent to return. A Nursing Facility resident generally cannot establish a new home property while residing in a facility since they would have never lived there and the new residence would not meet the definition of home property.

The value of your home property that is in another state outside of Louisiana is generally a countable asset.

Household Goods and Personal Effects. You can exclude the following items, regardless of value: one wedding ring and one engagement ring per individual, along with prosthetic devices, wheelchairs, hospital beds, dialysis machines, and other items required by a person's physical condition if they are not used extensively and primarily by the other members of your household.

A general exclusion of up to $2,000 applies to the total equity value of household goods and personal effects other than those excluded regardless of value.

Vehicles. One vehicle per household is excluded, regardless of its value, if anyone in the Medicaid applicant's household uses it for transportation. Medicaid assumes that your vehicle is used for transportation unless there is evidence to the contrary. This exclusion even applies to temporarily inoperable vehicles which are expected to be repaired and used for transportation within the next 12 months.

If you own more than one vehicle, the exclusion applies to the car with the greater equity value, regardless of which car is actually used. The equity value of all other vehicles, including inoperable vehicles and antique cars is counted. Medicaid uses the NADA "Blue Book" trade-in value at www.nadaguides.com.

Burial Contracts, Burial Funds, and Burial Spaces. A burial contract is countable if it is revocable or salable and conditions for its liquidation do not present a significant hardship. However, any portion of the burial contract that clearly represents the purchase of burial space may be excludable, and some or all of the remaining value may be excludable as burial funds. A burial contract is not countable if it cannot be revoked and cannot be sold without significant hardship

Burial Funds. Funds set aside for the burial expenses of the Medicaid applicant and his/her spouse may be excluded if those funds are clearly designated for the applicant or their spouse's burial expenses. A maximum exclusion of up to $10,000 each in funds set aside is allowed for the applicant and their spouse. This amount is reduced by the face value of your burial insurance which has no cash value.

Burial Spaces. A fully paid burial space or agreement that represents the purchase of a burial space held for your burial, your spouse's burial, or the burial of immediate family is excluded regardless of value.

What Are the Rules If You Are Married?

If you are married and receiving Medicaid benefits, some of your income can be paid to support your spouse.

The income and asset tests are significantly different if one spouse is in the nursing home (the "institutionalized spouse") and the other spouse stays at home or in the community (the "community spouse"). One rule that is rarely understood is that the income of the community spouse is never considered in determining eligibility for an institutionalized spouse.

Example. Mary Smith is applying for Medicaid. Her husband receives $4,000 of monthly pension and social security income. Mary receives $600 of monthly social security income. Bill's $4,000 of monthly income is not considered in determining Mary's Medicaid eligibility.

Ownership of income for each spouse is determined without regard to Louisiana community property laws. A spouse has full ownership of income paid to his name; a spouse has half ownership of income paid in the names of both spouses; and a spouse has pro rata ownership of income paid in the names of either one or both spouses and another individual.

The amount of the institutionalized spouse's income that a community spouse can keep on which to live is called the Maintenance Needs Allowance. Here is how it is calculated: Let's say Bill Smith has $2,000 of monthly income and his wife Mary has $1,000 of monthly income. Bill is in the nursing home and Mary wants to know if she can keep any of Bill's income.

We start by determining Bill's income ($2,100) and we deduct his personal needs allowance ($38) and we subtract his health insurance premiums ($150). The community spouse's liability totals $1,912.

Next, we subtract the spouse's monthly income ($1,000) from the Spouse's Maintenance Needs Allowance ($2,898.00 for the year 2013) to determine how much of Bill's income Mary can keep. In this case, Mary can keep $1,898 of Bill's monthly income, and the remaining $14 ($1,912 minus $1,898) is paid to the nursing home.

What Is the Asset Rule If You Are Married?

If you are single, in order to qualify for Medicaid you must have no more than $2,000 of countable assets.

The asset rules are very different for married couples when one spouse is in the nursing home (institutionalized spouse) and one spouse is at home (community spouse).

In Louisiana, a married couple can have as much as $117,240 (for 2014) in countable assets and the institutionalized spouse can qualify for Medicaid. This amount is called the Spousal Impoverishment-

Maintenance Needs and Resource Standards. It is defined as the maximum amount of the couple's combined countable resources that may be allocated to the community spouse.

A married couple's countable assets are defined as including the community spouse's assets, the institutionalized spouse's assets, and the couple's shared assets.

Example. In addition to their home and car, Bill and Mary Smith have countable assets totaling $175,000. Bill is in the nursing home. We know he can keep $2,000. Mary can keep $117,240. Bill will not qualify for Medicaid at this time because they have $55,760 "too much" in countable assets.

However, if Bill applied for Medicaid when he and Mary had countable assets totaling $90,000, he would qualify for Medicaid. Their total countable assets would be less than $117,240. However, the assets that are allocated to the institutionalized spouse that are in excess of $2,000 must be transferred to the community spouse in order for Bill to remain eligible.

Estate Recovery – Medicaid Can Take Your Home after You Die

The federal government has required the State of Louisiana (and all other states) to establish an estate recovery program. As a result, The Department of Health and Hospitals has established an estate recovery program for the purpose of recovering payments made to nursing homes on behalf of Medicaid recipients.

At the time that a Louisiana resident applies for Medicaid, the applicant shall be informed that federal law and regulations mandate estate recovery action by the state and that payments made by Medicaid may be subject to estate recovery.

Recovery can be made only after the death of the patient and his or her spouse. After the patient dies, Medicaid will serve a notice on the family or heirs of Medicaid's action.

Example. Bill Smith is in the nursing home and on Medicaid. His wife, Mary, lives in their home. Bill was eligible for Medicaid because their home was an exempt asset (for purposes of Medicaid eligibility) and their countable assets were less than $117,240. During Bill's stay in the nursing home, he spent $150,000 of Medicaid's funds. After both Bill and Mary die, Medicaid can force the home to be sold to be reimbursed for the Medicaid funds they spent for Bill.

Penalties for Transfers

Mary Jones would qualify for Medicaid except that she has a bank account with $61,000. Mary decides to give her daughter, Jane, a gift of $60,000. After the gift, Mary has only $1,000. Does Mary now qualify for Medicaid? Not a chance.

When you apply for Medicaid, the application asks you to list any transfers or gifts you have made to an individual or a trust in the last five years (or 60 months).

If a transfer is discovered during this 60 month look-back period, the applicant is disqualified for Medicaid until the penalty period expires. The penalty period is determined by dividing the value of the transfer by the Average Monthly Cost to Private Patients of Nursing Facility Services. For 2011, Louisiana has determined that the average cost of a nursing home stay is $4,000. So, if Mary made a transfer of $60,000, she would ineligible for Medicaid for 15 months ($60,000 transfer divided by $4,000 average nursing home cost).

When Does the Penalty Period Start?

For transfers on or after February 8, 2006, the penalty period starts when the individual is in the nursing home, has less than $2,000 of countable resources, and is determined by Medicaid to be eligible except for the occurrence of the transfer.

By now, you probably realize that Louisiana's Medicaid rules are complex. So let's take a look at some of the planning opportunities that are available.

Qualifying for Medicaid

Every Medicaid applicant's situation is unique. What may work for one person may not work for another. In developing a Medicaid plan, it is important that you work with someone knowledgeable in this complex area. The following are a few of the techniques often employed in assisting people in qualifying for Medicaid. The reason most people fail to qualify for Medicaid is that they have too many countable assets. So, most Medicaid Planning involves timely transfers of countable assets.

Owning Exempt Assets

Your house and your car are not countable. Certain burial contracts, burial funds, and burial spaces are also not countable. By simply transferring countable assets (such as cash) into non-countable assets, you can qualify for Medicaid.

Example. Bill and Mary Smith have a home valued at $150,000. There is $35,000 left on their mortgage. They drive an old car worth $2,000, and they have made no funeral arrangements. They have CDs at the bank totaling $90,000, and their checking and savings accounts total $70,000. Mary is entering the nursing home while Bill will stay at home. Mary presently does not qualify for Medicaid because their countable assets exceed $117,240. Their countable assets actually total $160,000. But if they use $35,000 of their cash to pay off their mortgage, purchase a better car for $20,000, and use $12,000 to prepay their funerals, their countable assets will be reduced to $93,000 and Bill will qualify for Medicaid.

Making Gifts

Making gifts to qualify for Medicaid is one of the most misunderstood aspects of Medicaid Planning. If you take the correct action to structure your estate properly and stay out of the nursing home for five years after you set things up, you can protect your entire estate. If, however, you are like many who do not think about Medicaid eligibility planning until just before a family member goes in the nursing home, you can still take certain actions to protect roughly half of your countable resources.

Planning in Advance

If you transfer your countable resources out of your name at least five years before you go into a nursing home, you can protect all of your assets. Many people do not want to put all of their assets into the names of their children. Read on to find out how you can keep some control over your assets by placing them into a particular type of irrevocable trust.

To Whom Should You Give Your Assets?

Good question. Your options include your children, a trust, or a combination of the two.

Most families who engage in Medicaid Planning agree up front that the money taken out of the parents' names will be "set aside" in an account or accounts for the children. Children informally agree they will not touch the money until after their parents die, and the children even informally agree they will spend the money on the parents, if necessary.

Unfortunately, things do not always work out as planned. Many times when parents give money to their children, the children end up spending it. Children have many reasons to spend it: they need it for a new truck or boat; they need to pay off credit card debt; they want a new home; they feel they deserve a vacation; they are influenced by their spouse; or it is just too easy to spend it. The children could also lose the money by getting divorced, getting sued, or owing the IRS or other creditors. The children might also die before the parents and then the family is stuck trying to retrieve the money from the child's heirs.

Trusts and Medicaid Planning

What is a trust? A trust, as defined by the Louisiana Trust Code, is the relationship resulting from the transfer of title to property to a person to be administered by him as a fiduciary for the benefit of another.

Example. John Boudreaux has four children. John wants to give his children a gift of $100,000, but he does not want them to spend it right away. John knows that if he gives $25,000 to each of his four children, at least three of them will spend it right away. John feels that his daughter, Jenny, is responsible and will act in accordance with John's wishes. So John establishes the Boudreaux Family Trust and names Jenny as the trustee of the trust. John would like to continue getting the interest from the $100,000, so he names himself as the income beneficiary of the trust. John would like the principal (the $100,000) to be distributed to his children after John's death. Jenny goes to the bank and sets up the Boudreaux Family Trust bank account. Only Jenny has signature authority over this account because she is the sole trustee. John then transfers $100,000 of his money to this trust account. Jenny thereafter, in her capacity as trustee, manages this money for the rest of John's lifetime, seeing to it that John continues to receive the interest as the income beneficiary of the trust, and Jenny distributes the principal to the four children (the principal beneficiaries) after John's death. Had John needed to move into a nursing home five years after setting this up, the $100,000 would not be considered a countable resource of John's for Medicaid eligibility purposes.

Trusts are a popular tool in Medicaid planning because, if established correctly, trusts can permit individuals and married couples to transfer assets out of their name, but retain control of the assets after they are transferred.

Many parents do not want to put their assets in their children's names because bad things can happen after the assets are transferred. Children might spend the assets, they might be influenced adversely by their spouses, children might get divorced and lose the assets, children may have creditor problems or problems with the IRS, or the children might get sued.

What If You Do Not Have Five Years?

Many people do not even think about qualifying for Medicaid until their loved one is on the doorstep of the nursing home. These people cannot wait five years to qualify, and they face the possibility of depleting their life savings before the five years runs out.

Special techniques are available that allow you to save half of your countable resources if you are either already in the nursing home or you are going into the nursing home soon. These techniques require working with someone who really understands the "ins and outs" of transferring assets out of your name and returning assets back to you.

Every few years the Medicaid eligibility rules change making it harder and harder to protect your assets and qualify for Medicaid.

Estate Planning in Louisiana

With America's population aging, the cost of care skyrocketing, and with less and less government funds available, it appears that it will be more important in the future to plan in advance for your potential long-term care nursing home stay.

Chapter 14

Successions and Probate
Handling Legal Matters When a Loved One Dies

When a loved one dies, there are many things, both legal and personal, that need to be handled. It is a difficult time for many families. An important legal matter that must occur whenever someone dies owning assets in their name is a succession.

What Is a Succession?

A succession is the process of transferring assets from the name of the person who died into the names of the appropriate heirs. Other states often call this process "probate," but in Louisiana, it is call a "succession."

The succession typically involves the family gathering information on what the decedent owned and bringing it to an attorney. The attorney then prepares numerous succession documents, including a detailed list of all the decedent's assets and liabilities, as well as a Judgment of Possession, which a judge signs ordering the transfer of assets out of the decedent's name and into the names of the heirs.

The attorney then files these documents at the local courthouse requesting that the Judge sign the appropriate Orders. Once the judge signs the Judgment of Possession, assets can be transferred.

Information to Gather

The succession process typically begins with the family gathering the necessary information on the decedent's assets that he or she owned at the date of his or her death. The information typically gathered includes copies of the following:

- Statements from banks and other financial institutions showing account balances and investments at or near the date of death;
- The Act of Sale of the residence and other Louisiana real estate showing the legal description of property owned by the decedent;
- Stock certificates if the decedent owned stock in certificate form;
- The Last Will and Testament (if one exists) of the decedent;
- Titles to vehicles, boats, and trailers owned by the decedent;
- Promissory Notes or Mortgages owned by the decedent;
- Mortgages the decedent owed;
- Funeral expenses; and
- Documentation showing other assets and debts that existed at the date of death.

Assets Not Included in the Succession

Certain assets you own are commonly referred to as "non-probate" assets. These are assets that go directly to a previously designated beneficiary upon the decedent's death. While these assets are typically not listed in the succession (unless the estate is the designated beneficiary), the attorney needs to be aware of these assets because they are included in the estate for federal estate tax purposes or they may have forced heirship consequences. Common non-probate assets include:

- Individual Retirement Accounts (IRAs)
- 401(k) accounts
- Life insurance
- Keogh accounts
- 403(b) accounts
- Annuities
- U.S. Savings Bonds titled in the name of the decedent "or" someone else
- Assets titled in the name of a trust

Once the attorney has all the relevant succession information, he can advise the family whether an "administration" is necessary. An administration occurs when the attorney prepares documents and presents them to the court so that an executor can be confirmed or an administrator can be appointed.

An administration is necessary when certain matters need to be tended to before the succession is completed. Common situations that require an administration include:

- A succession asset such as a house or other real estate, a vehicle, stock, or any other asset needs to be sold prior to completion of the succession;
- The executor or other third party needs access to the decedent's accounts to pay succession debts prior to the completion of the succession;
- Someone contests a succession matter.

If an administration is necessary, the court will sign an Order confirming that the person named in the Will shall serve as the executor, or the Judge will sign an Order appointing an administrator of the succession if no Last Will and Testament exists. The clerk of court will then issue "letters testamentary" (if an executor was named in the will), or "letters of administration" (if no Will exists and the judge appoints an administrator). This document puts third parties on notice that an executor has been confirmed or an administrator has been appointed.

Independent Administration

Recently the Louisiana Legislature authorized what is known as "independent administration." The traditional administration is often cumbersome, time-consuming, and expensive. For example, if an executor needed to take some action on behalf of the succession, such as pay a succession debt (for instance, a utility bill for the home), sell a succession vehicle, or even sell the decedent's home, the executor would have to petition the court for approval to pay the debt, sell the asset, or whatever other action needed to be taken by the executor. A judge would have to approve each of these actions in a written court order.

Paul A. Rabalais

Now, if the executor is confirmed as an "independent executor," he or she can take the necessary actions to administer the succession, such as pay succession debts and sell succession assets without having to obtain a judge's approval each time to do that.

How does an executor become an independent executor? There are two ways. First, the decedent could have appointed the executor in his Will as an independent executor. Second, if no such designation exists, then all the heirs can agree (in writing) to permit the executor (or the administrator if no Will exists) to serve as an independent executor or an independent administrator. Having an independent executor can make settling the estate much easier for all parties involved.

Many successions are concluded without an administration. Even though the decedent signed a Will and designated an executor, it may be unnecessary to go through the time and expense of having that person confirmed as the executor. When the succession is relatively free of debt and uncomplicated, the administration can be avoided. The succession documents are prepared and signed, and assets are transferred to the heirs without getting an executor confirmed or an administrator appointed.

The attorney will prepare all the succession documents, many of which are called "pleadings." The pleadings will be filed at the courthouse in the parish where the decedent lived (was domiciled) at the date of his death. The succession pleadings typically include:

- Affidavits of Death, Domicile and Heirship. These must be signed by two people familiar with the decedent's family circumstances. This is proof to the court of the decedent's death and family relationships.
- Detailed Descriptive List. This is a detailed list of all the succession assets and debts of the decedent as of the decedent's date of death.
- Petition for Possession. This is a succession pleading prepared by the attorney that lays out the relevant facts of the succession and requests that the Judge sign the Judgment of Possession.
- Petition for Probate of Testament (used when the decedent had signed a Last Will and Testament). This is a document filed with the signed Last Will and Testament of the decedent requesting that the Judge sign an Order stating that the Will is valid and ordering that it be followed.
- Judgment of Possession. This is often the most important document the Judge signs. This document, when signed by the Judge, orders third parties, such as banks, other financial institutions, transfer agents of corporations, the Office of Motor Vehicles, parish real estate offices, and others, to transfer assets that were formerly in the name of the decedent into the names of the appropriate heirs.

The heirs that the attorney represents will typically be asked to sign a document called a Verification in which the heirs "verify" that the information in the Petition for Possession is correct.

Transferring Assets to Heirs

After all the legal documents have been prepared, filed at the courthouse, and signed, it will be time to actually transfer the assets to the heirs.

Transferring Real Estate

In Louisiana, there are no deeds for real estate. If the decedent owned real estate, a certified copy of the Judgment of Possession will be recorded in the Conveyance Records of the parish where the property is located. This recording transfers title of the property to the heirs.

Transferring Bank Accounts

The heirs will bring a certified copy of the Judgment to the bank or other financial institutions, and the Judgment will order the banks to distribute the money or other assets to the heirs in the proportions as described in the Judgment. The bank or other financial institution will often require a certified death certificate or other information in addition to the certified copy of the Judgment of Possession. If the decedent owned Certificates of Deposit (CDs), there will typically be no penalty for early withdrawal if the CDs are cashed in pursuant to a Judgment of Possession.

Transferring Stock in Certificate Form

Let's say Mary owned 300 shares of ExxonMobil stock. In accordance with Mary's Will, the Judgment of Possession orders that those shares be divided equally among Mary's three children. ExxonMobil has a company that handles all stock transfers (known as the transfer agent). A certified copy of the Judgment of Possession and other paperwork the transfer agent requires is submitted to the transfer agent along with Mary's stock certificate, and the transfer agent sends the three children their new stock certificates showing that they each now own 100 shares of ExxonMobil stock.

Transferring Vehicles

The person or persons entitled to inherit the vehicle(s) by the Judgment of Possession will bring a certified copy of the Judgment of Possession to the Office of Motor Vehicles (OMV), and OMV will be ordered to issue a new vehicle title in the name(s) of the heir(s).

Does a Succession Take a Long Time?

It is reported in many national publications that probate takes many years to conclude. Many of these publications are also advocating the use of some probate avoidance tool.

In Louisiana, our probate/succession laws are simpler than the laws of many other states. Successions with absolutely no complications can take about two months to complete. An expedited timeline follows:

- January 1 – date of death
- January 15 – meet with attorney
- January 25 – supply all information requested to attorney

- February 15 – family meets with attorney to sign necessary documents
- February 20 – documents filed at courthouse
- February 28 – judge signs Judgment of Possession
- March 1-30 – assets transferred to heirs

Succession Delays

Many things can cause a delay in the completion of a succession. Typical reasons for delay include:

- The family or the attorney have difficulties in determining all the assets and liabilities of the succession;
- A personal representative (executor or administrator) needs to be confirmed or appointed to handle matters during the succession;
- Someone contests the succession or disagrees how the succession is being handled (this could cause completion of a succession to be delayed for years);
- Either the attorney, an heir or the family members in charge procrastinate;
- A federal estate tax return must be filed. This requires that certain succession assets be appraised and often requires that assets be sold to pay the tax. The federal estate tax return is due nine months after the death of the decedent and often the succession is often not completed until federal estate tax matters are concluded.

Succession Costs

Succession costs can vary from succession to succession, and from attorney to attorney. Attorney fees and court filing fees are a part of every succession. Some successions incur accounting fees and appraisal fees, federal estate tax, and other costs.

Some successions only include a house, a vehicle and perhaps a bank account or two. Other successions are much more extensive. When heirs choose to fight their differences out in court, the costs can be staggering.

Court filing fees vary from parish to parish. Attorney fees will vary from attorney to attorney. Unlike some other states, Louisiana has no statutory fee schedule. Louisiana attorneys are required to charge a "reasonable fee." Common examples of fee structures include:

- Hourly rate billing. The attorney will charge an hourly rate. This does not help clients because the client has no idea for how many hours the succession will be billed at the end;
- Fixed fee. This is where the attorney designates either a fixed amount or a fixed percentage of the estate to perform the services to be rendered. Clients like this because they know in advance the fee and the attorney is rewarded for his or her efficiency.

Whatever you do, make sure you have an agreement in writing with the attorney so that you will not be unpleasantly surprised later with an invoice that knocks your socks off.

Avoiding Probate

You can read in Chapter 12 of this book how you can create a revocable living trust and transfer your probate assets to your trust to avoid probate when you die.

In Louisiana, probate is generally becoming more expensive and more time-consuming. To completely avoid the requirement of a succession in Louisiana, you must not have any succession assets titled in your name when you die. There are typically two ways to do this.

First, you may own non-probate assets such as IRAs, 401(k)s and annuities. These assets pass directly to the designated beneficiaries and avoid the succession process.

Second, you may form a revocable living trust and transfer all of your succession assets to your trust before you die. Your trust will own your home, other real estate, and investment accounts. When you die, your assets are titled in the name of your trust. The succession process only governs the assets titled in your name.

Ignoring the Succession

Example. Bill and Mary were married for 40 years when Bill died. Mary continued to live in the home and drive the vehicles. She was the beneficiary of Bill's life insurance, and she had access to all their bank accounts, because the bank accounts were in their joint names. Four years go by after Bill's death. Mary never had the succession done, because she was told by her neighbor "she didn't need to do it."

Mary received bad advice from her neighbor. There are a number of reasons Mary should have seen a lawyer to complete the succession, including the fact that Mary will not be able to sell the home or vehicles because they are titled in the names of both Bill and Mary. Those assets cannot be sold until Bill's name is removed from the title.

Now, Mary cannot sell a vehicle and she cannot sell the home without completing the succession. In addition, Mary's family will have to complete *two* Louisiana successions when Mary dies – they will have to complete Bill's succession and they will have to complete Mary's succession.

Out-of-State Real Estate

The succession of a Louisiana resident not only governs all the financial accounts and other "movable" property, wherever located, but it governs the real estate located in Louisiana.

If a Louisiana resident owns real estate or mineral interests in another state, something called an ancillary probate will be required in that other state where they own property. Each state's ancillary probate laws are different, but an ancillary probate procedure typically includes filing a certified copy of the Last Will and Testament in that state, along with other paperwork required. This is typically done after the conclusion of the Louisiana succession. Often the family is required to hire an attorney in that other state to oversee that ancillary probate.

Owning significant real estate in other states can be a reason to transfer that property to an entity such as a limited liability company or a living trust, so that multiple ancillary probates can be avoided in states that have a burdensome probate process.

Contesting the Succession

Most successions are uncontested. The family member dies, the succession is handled, the property is transferred to the heirs, and families move on.

Some successions, however, are contested. It is unfortunate when heirs disagree. Often, no one wins. There is a common saying: "If you want to get to really know someone, share an inheritance with them."

There are a number of reasons why successions are contested. Some of them include:

- A person contests the validity or interpretation of the Last Will and Testament;
- An heir feels the executor is either not listing all the succession assets and debts properly, or the heir feels the executor is not acting appropriately;
- The heirs just do not like or trust each other (not a valid reason).

How to Contest a Succession

There are several ways a person can contest a succession:

Opposing the Appointment of Administrator

If you want to be notified when someone files an application to be appointed administrator, you can have your attorney petition the court so you will be notified when someone else petitions the court to be appointed the administrator. An administrator is often appointed when someone dies without a Last Will and Testament (so they did not appoint an executor). When more than one person wants to be the administrator, the court will give preference to the persons in the following order:

- The best qualified among the surviving spouse, or competent heirs or legatees;
- The best qualified of the nominees of the surviving spouse, or of the competent heirs or legatees;
- The best qualified of the creditors of the decedent or the estate, or a co-owner of immovable property with the decedent.

Contesting the Validity of the Will

When a person dies having signed a Will, the executor will usually have the attorney file the Will in the succession proceeding at the parish courthouse, and the judge will sign an Order stating that the Will is valid and ordering that it be followed.

If someone wants to question the validity of the Will, they will need to have their attorney prepare a petition stating the grounds of invalidity. When the validity of Wills is questioned, it is common for the person to question whether the deceased, at the time that the Will was written:

- had the ability to understand what he or she was doing; or
- was influenced by someone else so the document is not an accurate expression of the deceased's intentions.

Removing a Succession Representative

The succession representative can be either the executor of a Will or a court appointed administrator of an intestate (no Will) succession. If you think the succession representative should be removed, you can ask for a hearing where the succession representative must show why he should not be removed from office.

Duties and Rights of Succession Representative

The duties and rights of a succession representative include:

- He shall deposit all succession money in a succession bank account;
- He may invest the succession funds and make them productive;
- He may continue any business of the deceased;
- He may lease or sell succession property;
- He may pay succession debts.

Compensation of Succession Representative

If there is no provision in the Will to the contrary and no other agreement between the parties, the administrator or executor is allowed a fee of two and one-half percent of the succession assets. The court may increase the compensation upon a proper showing that the usual compensation is inadequate. In many successions, a family member is the executor or administrator, and that family member may waive this fee either because they are willing to do it for free because they are an heir and it is a family matter, or since the succession representative's fee is subject to income tax, he feels satisfied receiving his inheritance, which is not subject to income tax.

Conclusion

A Louisiana succession is required when a person dies and the individual had property titled in his or name on their date of death. The succession is the process of transferring assets from the deceased's name to the heirs. A succession typically involves the following:

- You gather documentation regarding the deceased's assets and deliver it to your succession attorney;
- Uncomplicated successions do not require an administration (the court appointment of an executor or administrator). If an administration is necessary, it is much easier if it is an "independent" administration;
- Your succession attorney will file documents at the parish courthouse where the decedent was

domiciled. A judge will sign a court order requiring third parties to transfer assets to the proper heirs;

- Many individuals choose to ultimately distribute their estate through a living trust to avoid the costs and delays associated with the court-supervised succession procedure. Couples can avoid two probates by properly setting up a living trust;
- There are strict rules regarding how Wills and successions are to be handled. If an interested party has sufficient legal authority, he or she can contest the way a succession is being handled.

Chapter 15

Non-probate Assets
These Are Important and Often Overlooked

It is likely that you own non-probate assets. Non-probate assets are assets that do not pass pursuant to your Will when you die. Common non-probate assets include your retirement accounts (such as your IRA or 401(k)), life insurance, and annuities. It is important that you monitor these assets during your lifetime and properly designate your beneficiaries.

Maybe you are like some people who have the bulk of their life savings in non-probate assets. Perhaps you worked for a company that had a 401(k) plan. When you retired, you rolled your 401(k) plan assets into an individual retirement account (IRA). You take monthly or annual distributions from your IRA to pay for your retirement. Your other assets include your home and some smaller accounts outside of your IRA.

Perhaps you are married and your spouse has children from a prior marriage. You set up a Will and designate that all your assets go to your children when you die. However, you fail to realize that your spouse is named as the primary beneficiary of your IRA – your biggest asset by far. When you die, your children do not get any of your IRA, even though you wrote a Will designating that your children receive all of your assets when you die. What is worse is that after your death, your spouse can roll your IRA over into his or her IRA so when they later dies their IRA goes to his or her children (or perhaps his or her new spouse).

For many people, properly designating beneficiaries on non-probate assets is just as important, if not more important, than creating a Will or revocable living trust. Failing to properly designate your beneficiaries on non-probate assets could result in your life savings being transferred to people other than those closest to you.

The following are examples of common non-probate assets along with what you can do to make sure that your wishes are carried out.

Retirement Accounts

Retirement accounts include Keogh pensions, profit-sharing or stock bonus plans qualified under the Internal Revenue Code, an individual retirement account (IRA), a Roth IRA, or a tax-sheltered annuity.

Traditional families often do not encounter problems with IRAs. Traditional families are those where the two parents had children together, and all members of the family agree that when one spouse dies, the surviving spouse should own the IRA, and when the surviving spouse dies, the IRA will be divided equally among the children. The spouse is typically named as the primary beneficiary and all of their children are named as the contingent beneficiaries.

The problem occurs when the family circumstances vary from the traditional. Often, individuals go into great detail when having their Wills prepared so that spouses, children, and other loved ones are protected. But little, if any, attention is given to the beneficiary designation forms on the retirement accounts.

Example. Jack had two children from his prior marriage. Jack is currently married to Rachel. Jack sets up his Will so Rachel gets the lifetime usufruct of Jack's entire estate, and Jack names his two children as the naked owners. Jack has an IRA valued at $600,000, while his other assets (his interest in the home and other financial accounts) total $300,000. When Jack died, Rachel received Jack's entire $600,000 IRA, because she was the primary beneficiary while Jack's children were merely the contingent beneficiaries. Rachel received the usufruct of the $300,000 of assets that passed pursuant to Jack's Will. Rachel will one day be accountable to Jack's children for the $300,000 of assets over which she has usufruct. Rachel is free to do whatever she wants with his IRA, including leave it to her children (not Jack's children) or leave it to the husband she marries after Jack dies.

If Jack wanted his children to benefit from his IRA, he could have named them as primary beneficiaries of part or all of the IRA (for example, 25% to each of his two children and 50% to his wife, Rachel), or he could have named a trust as the primary beneficiary of his IRA. The trust instrument would likely have allowed

Rachel to use the IRA during her lifetime and then at her death, the remainder of the IRA in trust would go back to Jack's children (not Rachel's beneficiaries).

If you name a trust as the beneficiary of your IRA, be aware that there are numerous hurdles involving income tax, minimum required distributions, and trust accounting, but doing it properly can allow you to provide for all of your loved ones regardless of your family circumstances.

Life Insurance

Life insurance proceeds, generally, are income tax free to the beneficiaries. Life insurance is also a non-probate asset. When you purchase a life insurance policy, you are asked to name a beneficiary on the life insurance company's beneficiary designation form. Even if your Will states that you want your life insurance to go to your children or your spouse, the life insurance company will only pay the proceeds to the beneficiary who is designated on the beneficiary designation form, regardless of what your Will provides.

Similar to the way your retirement accounts should be handled, if you want your spouse to benefit from your life insurance, and you want to designate who gets the remaining funds when your spouse dies, you should consider naming a trust as the beneficiary. Otherwise, your spouse will be free to leave that money to whomever he or she wishes (which may or may not be the same people you would want to have it).

Annuities

Annuities also are distributed after your death to the named beneficiaries. If you own annuities, make certain that you have properly documented your beneficiaries. Many annuity owners die without fully understanding how the non-probate assets are to be distributed. Some of these people may be rolling over in their graves right now.

Conclusion

Failing to properly designate beneficiaries on non-probate assets is one of the costliest and most-overlooked aspects of estate planning.

If you have non-probate assets such as retirement accounts, life insurance, and annuities, consider the following:

- Review your primary and contingent beneficiaries regularly;
- If you are married and you have children from a prior marriage, consider designating a trust as the beneficiary of non-probate assets. This will allow you, for example, to provide for your surviving spouse and also provide who benefits from the trust assets after the death of your surviving spouse.;
- You can designate multiple primary beneficiaries. For example, your spouse may be a 50% beneficiary, and your children may each be 25% beneficiaries;

- If you name a trust or someone other than your spouse as the primary beneficiary of your retirement accounts, be aware of the income tax consequences as well as the often-changing rules regarding minimum required distributions.

Chapter 16

Estate Planning Letter of Last Instructions
Make It Easy for Your Loved Ones

While it is important that the proper estate planning legal documents be in place, it is also important that other informal items be properly documented.

Examples of additional items that should be documented include:

- Your wishes regarding your personal effects
- Who to notify upon your death
- Your desired funeral arrangements
- The location of your personal papers
- Access to your vehicle titles and registration
- Recent statements of bank and investment accounts
- Location and key to safe deposit boxes
- List of your debts
- Property descriptions for real estate you own
- List of survivor's benefits

Personal Effects

The disposition of your personal effects, such as furniture, jewelry, art, guns, tools, clothing, photographs, and other non-titled assets can be one of the most difficult things for your heirs to handle. While it is easy for your two children to divide up the money that is in your bank account, it is not so simple for children to divide your family portraits or other family heirlooms.

Disposing of your personal effects can be done generally in one of two ways. First, you could specify who you want to get your personal items in your Last Will and Testament. This is often not recommended, because you have to include a detailed list of your personal effects in your Will, and if you want to add, delete, or change one of these bequests, you have to go through the formal process of changing your Will.

An alternative to listing your personal effects in your Will is to create a less formal set of instructions to your heirs where you personally and in writing, let them know how you want your personal effects distributed. It may be in your own handwriting or it might be something you type on the computer. The idea is not to make a formal document, but an informal request to your heirs about how to divide these items that often do not have significant market value, but have tremendous sentimental value.

Example. Maria has a daughter and two sons. In her Will, she provided that all of her assets were to go equally to her three children. After she had her Will prepared by an attorney, she sat down and prepared a letter to her children stating which personal effects she wanted to go to each child and grandchild. While this informal letter was not a valid legal document, Maria's children honored her requests after she died and divided all of her personal effects in accordance with her wishes.

While this informal method of distributing personal effects is simple and works particularly well when all the heirs are close, be aware that if you want to make absolutely certain your wishes are followed, you need to consider expressly stating your wishes in your Will.

List of Assets

You should take certain actions now so your loved ones will have an easier time settling your affairs when you are gone. One of the things you can do is complete a detailed list of your assets and liabilities. Keep this list with your other important estate planning documents and update it annually. When you die, your family will have to produce this information to the succession attorney, and it will be much easier for them to access the necessary information if you have left them a complete list of your assets and debts. Your list of assets should include:

- Real estate. A legal description of each piece of real estate that you own. The complete legal description can be found on the Act of Sale or Act of Mortgage from when you purchased or otherwise acquired the property.
- Bank accounts. An itemized listing of bank accounts in which you have an ownership interest.

- Investments. A listing of investment accounts and copies of stock certificates you own.
- Vehicles. Copies of titles to your cars, boats, etc.
- Debts. A list of your creditors, such as mortgage companies, banks, and credit card companies.
- Other important information. Also include with this list of assets information regarding your funeral arrangements, the location and contents of your safe deposit boxes, and the location and status of any life insurance policies of which you are the owner or the insured.

Conclusion

Properly documenting your assets during your lifetime and informally providing for the disposition of your personal effects may be just as important as having the proper estate planning legal documents in place.

Make a list of your assets and debts and keep it updated annually. Let the person you named as executor in your Will know how to access this information.

If you want to avoid a squabble among your heirs over your personal effects such as family pictures, furniture, jewelry, and other personal items, write an informal letter to them instructing them on how to divide those items. When they see that you have documented what you wanted, they will be inclined to honor your wishes.

Chapter 17

Get Started
It's Not as Painful as You Might Think

Because of the uncertainties of life, it is never too early to begin estate planning. Having a proper estate plan can be one of the best things you can do for the loved ones you leave behind.

Estate planning is not painful. You will not get pricked or prodded. Once your estate planning is up to date, you will have peace of mind knowing that you have done what is necessary to have your affairs in order.

To get started, take the following steps:

Find an Attorney

There are a number of different ways you can find a competent attorney. Some of these include:

- Ask your friends, neighbors, and relatives who they know who could help you with your estate plan. If they had a good experience using a certain attorney, it is likely that you will also have a good experience.

- Many attorneys are listed in the telephone book or on the internet. While a referral from a trusted source is the best bet, you will be able to find a number of attorneys in the yellow pages or on the internet. Make sure they list estate planning as a significant part of their practice.
- These days, lawyers specialize. Estate planning can be a complex field. Just as you would search for a specialist to assist you with a particular medical problem, you will want to find an attorney who specializes in estate planning. The State of Louisiana recognizes estate planning and administration as a specialty. For a lawyer to claim he is a specialist in estate planning, he must have passed a test administered by the state bar, and he must obtain additional continuing education credits annually.

Meet with the Attorney

Many attorneys will offer to meet with you in an initial meeting without you incurring any cost. This is a great way for you to get to know the attorney and to find out whether you would want to work with him or her. You will be able to ask questions, and the attorney will likely make certain recommendations to you in order to complete your estate plan. The attorney should also be able to give you a quote or an estimate regarding the fees you will be required to pay. Do not ever retain an attorney without first having a thorough understanding of how you will be charged.

Paul A. Rabalais

Be Prepared

Once you have located your attorney, it is helpful if you provide him with a general list of your assets and their values. The attorney will be able to determine if there is any special planning that will be necessary to reduce potential tax.

When you meet with the attorney, be prepared to answer the following questions:

If you are married, how do you want to leave assets to your spouse? Do you want to leave your spouse full ownership or do you want to leave your spouse usufruct? Or perhaps you want to leave assets in trust for your spouse.

How do you want to leave assets to your children? Do you want to leave assets to them outright or in trust? If you leave assets to your children in trust, who will be the trustee and under what circumstances can your children use the trust principal?

Do you want to leave a bequest to your grandchildren? Some grandparents want to leave a bequest to their grandchildren, while others want to leave it all to their children. There is no right or wrong way to do it.

Do you want to leave a bequest to charity?

Who will serve as your executor? If you are married, you may want your spouse to be your executor, and you may want an adult child to be your alternate executor.

Estate Planning in Louisiana

Who do you want to handle your financial affairs for you during your lifetime in the event you cannot do it for yourself?

Who do you want making your medical decisions for you if you are unable?

Do you want to sign a living will declaration whereby you declare your intentions regarding life support machines?

Once you answer these and other questions, your attorney should have the necessary information to draft the appropriate estate planning documents. These documents typically include your Last Will and Testament, power of attorney, health care power of attorney, living will declaration, and perhaps trusts or other documents.

Once you are satisfied with the documents, you will sign them in the presence of a notary (usually your attorney) and two witnesses.

In addition to signing the necessary estate planning documents that are customized by your attorney, you also need to make certain all necessary beneficiary designation forms are properly completed.

Storing Your Estate Planning Documents

Keep your signed, original Last Will and Testament in a safe place. Some people keep their Will in a bank safe deposit box, while other people keep their Will in their home. The attorney should keep a photocopy of your Will.

Let your executor know where your original Will is located. If you keep it in a safe deposit box, make sure you complete the necessary paperwork at the bank so your trusted friend or relative can access the box after your death without having to get the courts involved.

Review Your Estate Plan

Do not make the common mistake of completing your estate plan, and then having it collect dust for many years. Your circumstances are likely to change over the years and your estate plan needs to keep up with your changing circumstances. Meet with your attorney about every three to five years, or more often if any of the following occur:

- One of your heirs has died
- There is a significant change in the value of what you own
- You change your mind about how you will leave your assets to your heirs
- You want to change your executor or you want to change your power of attorney
- You discover there is a change in the law that may affect you
- You get married or divorced
- You incur a life-threatening illness
- You move into or out of the state

Conclusion

In estate planning, Louisiana's laws are far different from the laws of all the other states. To complete and maintain a proper estate plan, do the following:

- Find an attorney who you are comfortable with – particularly one who specializes in the complex field of estate planning.
- Be prepared to provide the attorney with information about what you own.
- Be prepared to answer the attorney's questions about how you want to leave your assets, as well as questions regarding who you would want making important financial and medical decisions for you when you are unable to make them for yourself.
- Make certain you execute the proper estate planning legal documents as well as beneficiary designation forms.
- Store your documents so your trusted friends, relatives, and advisors have access to them upon your disability or your death.
- Review your estate plan periodically so it can be updated as your circumstances change.

Congratulations! You should now be informed enough so you can undertake the important task of estate planning. Once you have an up-to-date estate plan, you will have peace of mind knowing you have done what is necessary to protect yourself and your loved ones, and you can continue to enjoy your life!

Glossary

Administrator – the person appointed by the court whose duty it is to collect, preserve and manage the property of a succession. The court often appoints an administrator when a decedent had no Last Will and Testament

Collation – the return of gifted assets by an heir to a succession in order that succession property can be divided equally. People often provide in their Wills that lifetime gifts are exempt from collation

Community Property – property acquired by spouses during their marriage in which each spouse owns an undivided one-half interest. Louisiana is a community property state

Estate Administration – the process of settling an estate after someone dies

Executor – the person you designate in your Last Will and Testament who will work with the attorney to settle your estate

Estate Planning – the process of arranging your affairs to that upon your death or disability, your estate will be managed efficiently by the people you trust, and there will be minimal costs of succession, tax, long-term care, or other costs

Estate Tax – the tax your estate must pay to the federal government if your net estate exceeds the applicable estate tax exemption at your death

Estate Planning in Louisiana

Forced Heirship – the concept in Louisiana that your children that are either (1) age 23 or younger at your death; or (2) unable to manage their own affairs regardless of their age, are automatically entitled to inherit from you, regardless of what you write in your Last Will and Testament

Gift Tax – tax you must pay to the state or federal government for making a gift for the benefit of another person

Heir – a person who inherits from you when you do not have a Last Will and Testament. The people you name in your Will to inherit from you, in Louisiana, are called legatees

Independent Executor – your executor who is allowed to act pursuant to a simpler probate process because you either authorized it in your Will or all of your heirs agreed to allow the executor to serve as an independent executor. Independent executors typically do not require the court authorization to act that is otherwise required of executors

Inheritance Tax – the amount of tax owed to the State of Louisiana by your heirs when they inherit from you. This tax no longer exists.

Intestate Laws – the laws that dictate who inherits your assets if you die without a valid Last Will and Testament

Last Will and Testament – a legal document naming your executor and describing, among other things, who is entitled to your assets when you die

Legatee – a person you name in your Last Will and Testament who will inherit from you

Legitime – the amount of your estate that you must leave to your forced heirs

Living Trust – a trust that you establish during your lifetime

Living Will – a document whereby you express your intentions regarding the withdrawal or withholding of life support systems

Marital Portion – the amount that a surviving spouse is entitled to claim when the surviving spouse is "poor" in comparison to the deceased spouse who was "rich"

Marriage Contract – a document two individuals sign, typically prior to marriage, in order to deviate from the community property rules.

Medicaid – the federal and state program that will pay for all or a portion of your nursing home care if you meet the Medicaid eligibility requirements

Medicaid Planning – the process of taking advantage of legal strategies to protect your estate in the event you need long-term care in a nursing home

Estate Planning in Louisiana

Medicare – completely different from Medicaid. Medicare is health insurance for most senior citizens, paying most of the cost for surgeries, doctor visits, and other medical expenses

Naked Owner – the person who is entitled to ownership of assets at the termination of the usufruct

Non-probate assets – assets that are not listed in a succession, such as qualified retirement plans, individual retirement accounts, life insurance, and annuities

Notarial Will – one of two forms of valid Wills in Louisiana. Most wills in Louisiana are notarial wills. Notarial wills are typically typed, they have certain required language, they are signed on every page, and they are formally notarized and witnessed

Olographic Will – one of two forms of valid Wills in Louisiana. It is entirely in your own handwriting, signed and dated. Olographic wills are not recommended, because lay people typically do not have the expertise to prepare such an important legal document as their Last Will and Testament

Power of Attorney – a document you sign authorizing another to act for you during your lifetime

Probate – the court-supervised process of transferring your assets to your heirs or legatees after your death. Also known as "succession" in Louisiana

Paul A. Rabalais

Revocable Living Trust – a type of trust you create during your lifetime, whereby you are the trustee and beneficiary during your lifetime, and you provide who the beneficiaries are at your death. Often used as a Will substitute to avoid probate

Separate Property – property that you own that is not community property with your spouse. Common examples of separate property are property you acquired before you married, property you inherited, and property that was given to you by someone else.

Settlor – a person who creates a trust.

Succession – the court-supervised process of transferring your assets to your heirs after you die. In other states, it is called probate.

Testamentary Trust – a trust, the terms of which are stated in your Last Will and Testament. Parents with minor children often establish testamentary trusts in their Wills.

Trust – a relationship resulting from the transfer of title to property to a person (trustee) to be administered for the benefit of another (beneficiary)

Trustee – the person who manages the assets of the trust for the beneficiaries.

Tutor – the legal guardian of a child under the age of eighteen

Usufruct – a right of limited duration on the property of another. A spouse often leaves his or her surviving spouse the usufruct of his or her estate, and names the children as the naked owners

Usufructuary – the person who owns the usufruct

Will – also known as your Last Will and Testament. Your Will is the important document that you sign which leaves your estate to your loved ones, names your executor, and provides for many other aspects regarding the settling of your estate

To schedule a no-cost initial visit with an attorney from Rabalais Law, or to attend a free seminar or webinar, please visit our website or contact us at any of our offices.

Rabalais Law
(A Professional Corporation)
www.EstatePlanningInLouisiana.com
e-mail: paul@rabalaislaw.com
Toll free: (866) 491-3884

Office locations:

Alexandria
Baton Rouge
Houma
Lafayette
Lake Charles
Mandeville
Monroe
New Orleans
Shreveport

In Their Own Words...

Testimonials from satisfied clients of Rabalais Law:

My wife, Rebecca, and I first attended an Estate Planning Seminar presented by Paul Rabalais in September 2003. Since then, Paul has done an exceptional job in guiding our family through (3) separate family losses. He is very professional, extremely knowledgeable in Louisiana Tax laws and assisted us in an estate plan that is most beneficial to our family. He has a staff that is also very courteous, knowledgeable and supports Rabalais Law in a very professional way. We have recommended Paul to several of our family and friends and would highly recommend him to anyone who is considering an estate plan."

Glenn and Rebecca Nijoka
Baton Rouge, Louisiana

Both you and the office staff were courteous and accommodating. You did a great job of first asking questions and then explaining the options available. Recommendations were made based upon our personal situation. Vanda and I walked away very happy with a plan in place for each other and our children.

Rann and Vanda Upton
Mandeville, Louisiana

Paul Rabalais and his staff were great! Paul's knowledge and expertise in Louisiana estate law made the process of preparing these important family documents quick and easy. His manner made the discussion of sensitive topics feel perfectly natural. It was a big relief to us to get our affairs in order and remove a big source of worry about our children's well-being.

Thanks,
Bernardo and Lacey Corripio
Baton Rouge, Louisiana

We had the pleasure of being referred to Rabalais Law to discuss executing a will. Our situation was unique with a combined family consisting of 13 children. Paul and his staff worked with us to properly address all of our needs. We found the staff to be thorough, knowledgeable and extremely professional. Their communication with various drafts was accurate and very prompt. The completed paperwork consisted of a neatly packaged document that allows for all of our desires to be properly passed on to our family when we pass away. We would highly recommend Rabalais Law and will use them again in the future for any of our estate concerns.

Clyde and Karen Messenger
Denham Springs, Louisiana

We found the staff to be very friendly, professional, and knowledgeable. We would gladly recommend this firm.

Glenn and Mary Orr
Denham Springs, Louisiana

Changes in Louisiana law and changes in our own personal situations caused us recently to execute changes in our estate planning documents: Last Will & Testament, Property Power of Attorney, Health Care Power of Attorney and Living Will. All these documents were drawn up to meet our specific needs through the services of Rabalais Law. The entire process turned out to be unexpectedly easy for us because everyone in the firm was consistently understanding, patient, friendly and obviously determined to ensure that we understood what we were doing and that we would be pleased with the finished products. We were comfortable working with those in Rabalais Law as we would have been getting the same professional services from an old friend or family member.

Mr. Rabalais keeps us informed and up-to-date on current developments through e-mails and on-line seminars. Without reservation we heartily recommend Rabalais Law to anyone wanting estate planning expertise with friendly, courteous attention to one's specific needs.

Joseph and Hilda Pilcher
Kenner, Louisiana

We attended our first Rabalais seminar in 1997, established a will-based estate plan in 2004, and changed to the Revocable Trust plan in 2011. We've always found Paul and his staff to be very knowledgeable and personable in incorporating our desires into the documents that will govern our lives and estate in times when we may be unable to do so.

Ralph and Fran Cambre
Slidell, Louisiana

Thanks for making the whole estate planning process easy to understand. You and your staff are so helpful and friendly. Now we wonder why we waited so long to get this taken care of.

Gaylon and Carolyn Nicholson
Lafayette, Louisiana

Paul and his staff made the entire process of setting up a revocable trust easy and quick. We had put off doing this feeling it would be a jumble of legal issues. Not so! Thanks to Paul and Catherine Martinez we sailed through the process without a hitch.

Many Thanks,
Hunter and Terri Willett
Baton Rouge, Louisiana

What a great pleasure to meet you and your staff! We had so many questions about updating our will and you helped reassure us of all these issues. Your professional, yet personable mannerisms in conducting business truly helped us as well. We feel so much more confident about our future desires for our own lives, as well as those of our children. Thank you for your thoughtfulness and concern. We are so pleased with the prepared and completed portfolio containing these papers. Thank you again.

Harlen and Elizabeth Judice
Vinton, Louisiana

My late husband and I came to use the services of Mr. Rabalais a few years prior to my husband's death in 2005. I have been quite pleased with the compassionate and knowledgeable manner in which Mr. Rabalais handled our Wills before my husband's death and how quickly he finalized the probate procedure. Mr. Rabalais is always available when I need his services in regard to estate planning matters. I highly recommend his services to anyone.

Jeanette Pendley
Baton Rouge, Louisiana

What a pleasant surprise! I fully expected a rather painful process while getting through our estate planning, wills, etc. (which may explain my reluctance to have it done.) From the first visit, however, up until our receipt of your most impressive portfolio of our estate affairs, we were confident that we had placed our trust in the right person. I believe that our confidence was due to your skill as a listener and communicator, and your apparent knowledge of Louisiana Tax Laws in general, and how specific laws would affect us, in particular. It was a most positive experience for us, Paul, and I am glad we were led to you for help.

Ferol and Elizabeth Simoneaux
Destrehan, Louisiana

My husband I had put off doing our will and medical directives for several years thinking it would be a long, complicated and tedious process. But, thanks to the Rabalais Office Staff we've completed all of our legal paperwork and directions for our loved ones in one session! We've made these hard decisions concerning end of life matters so our children will not have to do this!

Mertile and Patricia Settoon
Plaquemine, Louisiana

I just wanted to add my thanks to you for the help you gave me as my attorney and you did a phenomenal job of my estate planning.

Lois S. Matherne
Baton Rouge, Louisiana

You and your staff are very detailed and efficient. I am proud to recommend you to my friends and anyone who needs your service.

James Adams, Sr.
Baton Rouge, Louisiana

We were very pleased with Paul's services! He explained everything to us in a language we could understand. He answered all of our questions and made sure we understood all of it. We will highly recommend him to others.

Hushel and Frances Bordelon
Washington, Louisiana

Rabalais Law is top notch. Paul's advice is precise and easy to understand. He ensured our goals are set in place and made the estate planning process as easy as possible. They get my highest rating.

Stephen P. and Margaret Jones
Baton Rouge, Louisiana